A Village School

Other books published by the Froyle Archive

Froyle, 100 Years of Memories

A Village School

by Annette Booth & Nora Jupe

The Froyle Archive
www.froyle.demon.co.uk

First published in 2003 by
The Froyle Archive
Little Greystones, Lower Froyle
Alton, Hampshire
GU34 4LJ

schooldays@froyle.demon.co.uk

ISBN 0 9545460 0 8

Printed in the United Kingdom by Biddles Ltd

Contents

This book is dedicated to all those people
who have passed through the doors of Froyle School

I would like to thank Tony Jupe for allowing me access to his late wife's
documents, and my husband, Chris, for his expertise in publishing this book

Foreword

The story of a village school must, of necessity, be the story of the people of the village. This latest book by Annette Booth is no exception.

Founded in the middle of the nineteenth century through the benevolence of the Lord of the Manor, as were so many other village schools, Froyle School flourished for over a hundred years; bringing together children to form lasting friendships and who, in later years, would become the mainstay of the village.

Names appearing in the first Attendance Register of 1868 still live on 135 years later. Descendants of pupils who appear on this Register and, indeed, pupils themselves, who attended the school in its later days, have been only too glad to tell of their experiences, and the experiences of their forebears; many of them happy, but some woeful and even painful!

Added to this Annette has had access to very detailed log books which give a fascinating glimpse into the day-to-day running of the school and the problems facing the 'Master'. As will be seen, this has involved her in much painstaking research to extract those parts which will add to her story and will be of particular interest to readers in the twenty-first century.

A delightful book for anybody interested in English country life.

John Willcocks

John Willcocks,
Last Chairman of the Governors of Froyle Primary School

Introduction

In 1986, owing to falling numbers, the primary school in the North East Hampshire village of Froyle closed and its twenty two children transferred to nearby Bentley School. The Headteacher, Mrs Nora Jupe, wanted the school to "go out with a bang", and so, along with a number of other events, a 'School Farewell Occasion' was organised, comprising an exhibition of photographs and memorabilia charting the school's 118 years of educating the children of Froyle. My husband, Chris, and I mounted that exhibition and much of the material used then has formed the basis of this book.

Nora Jupe retired with the closure of the school and, in her retirement, researched and wrote a history of Froyle School from the log books of the time. It was published, privately, ten years ago, under the title, "12 x 10, A History of Froyle School".

Sadly, Nora passed away in 1999, but I was delighted when her husband, Tony, agreed that I might incorporate her work into this title. I have interspersed her writings with additional material, the actual log book entries, photographs from the Froyle Archive, and the memories of children and staff who attended Froyle School.

Throughout the text, entries from the log books, as well as H.M.I. Reports, have been printed in italics. Where schoolgirl memories have been included, I have used the girls' maiden names, so that they might still be recognised by any school friend who might have lost touch over the years!

I would like to thank all those Froyle people who have allowed me to use their photographs and who have shared their memories with me, some of which, I hope they will appreciate, I simply couldn't use!! I have to say, I rather like the comments of more than one 'lad' who, when asked what his unhappiest memory of Froyle School was, said, "Attending!" And yes, you've guessed it, his happiest memory was, "Leaving!"

Seriously though, the overwhelming impression I received, both from research and from talking to everyone associated with Froyle School, was that it was a happy place, which played a pivotal role in the community for over a century. It is sadly missed, to this day.

Annette Booth
Froyle, 2003

Pre·School

The land on which Froyle School would eventually be built formed the kitchen garden of this house in Upper Froyle. When this drawing was commisioned in 1836 the house was owned by Miss Mary Moody and her sister. It was purchased in 1860 by Sir Thomas Combe Miller following the death of the last surviving sister, pulled down and the land incorporated into Froyle Park.

1

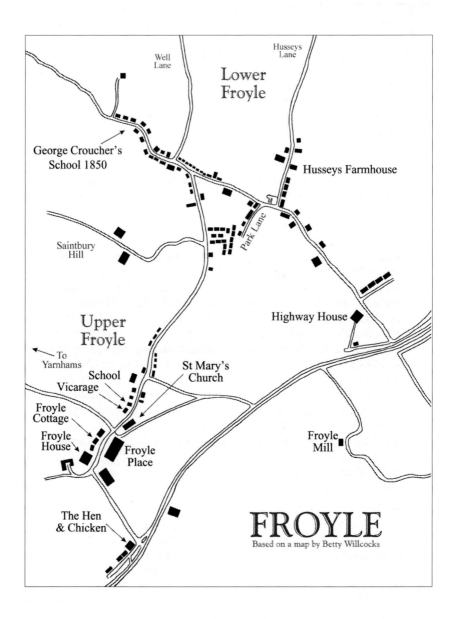

FROYLE

Based on a map by Betty Willcocks

THE village school in Froyle opened in the latter half of the nineteenth century, but how had children been educated in the village before that time? Let's begin by familiarising ourselves with this small community, tucked away in the north east corner of Hampshire, four miles from the market town of Alton. As you can see from the map opposite, the village is made up of two parts, Upper Froyle, centred around St Mary's Church and Froyle Place, and Lower Froyle, which grew up around the farms.

In 1859 William White wrote in his 'History, Gazetteer and Directory of Hampshire and the Isle of Wight',

> "*FROYLE is a pleasant, well-built village, on the north side of the fertile vale of the river Wey, two miles W. of Bentley Station, and four miles N.E. by E. of Alton. Its parish contains 826 souls and 3618 acres of land, including the village of LOWER FROYLE, more than a mile N.E. of the Church, and several scattered farm houses etc. There are hop yards on all the farms. FROYLE HOUSE, a neat mansion with pleasant grounds, is the seat of Henry Burningham, Esq.; and HIGHWAY HOUSE, another handsome mansion, is the seat of Mrs Watkins; but the Rev. Sir Thomas Combe Miller, Bart., is Lord of the Manor, owner of a great part of the parish, and patron and incumbent of the vicarage, which is valued at £254. He is seated at FROYLE PLACE, a neat mansion in a finely wooded park, adjoining the grounds of the before-mentioned mansions. He is the fifth baronet of his family. The first baronet was M.P. for Chichester in 1688 and 1690, and was created a baronet in 1705. The second and third baronets also represented Chichester in parliament. The present baronet was born in 1803, and his son and heir, Charles Hayes Miller, Esq., in 1829. The Church (St Mary's) is a neat structure, in the early English style, with a tower and six bells. It was restored in 1842, by the present patron and incumbent. The Vicarage House is occupied by the curate. In Domesday Book, Froli is noticed as being in 'Neatham Hundred', and as belonging to the Abbess of St Mary's, Winchester. There are Post Offices in Upper and Lower Froyle.*

In the 21st century the village is home to some 600 people, many of whom either commute to the city or work from home in what have become 'techno-cottages'. Froyle Place is now part of the Treloar School for disabled children, offering boarding and day education to 7-16 year olds and day placement for 5-7 year-olds. Students come from all over Britain and the school has a reputation second to none. Since 1980 the village has lost its vicarage, two shops and post offices, a public house, the Methodist church and the village school, hence this book! But it is not a dying community; it is vibrant and caring, always looking to the future, but remembering its past with pride.

Now that we have set the scene, so to speak, let's return to the subject of education. The very earliest mention we can find has come in a letter written by a John Knight to his brother Stephen, who lived at Chawton Manor, near Alton, regarding Stephen's son, whom he apparently treated as his heir. In the letter, dated 10th January 1616, John writes "The imperfection you speak of in your son's speech, I have not at any time observed, butt that in speaking he doth lyspe. I hope he be long since come from you and att Froyle." However, in May of the same year he writes of his intention to move his nephew to a schoolmaster at Basingstoke, "his (the nephew's) usage at Froyle was not to my liking".

A copy of a will which has come to light informs us that, in May 1751, one James Marshall bequeathed £5 per annum to teach poor children of Froyle to read and write.

> *"I give an annuity or charge of five pounds a year to this intent, that the said Churchwardens and Overseers and their successors do cause so many poor children that do not receive alms on the parish of Froyle aforesaid to be instructed to read and write."*

There was, however, no known 'education centre' in the village at this time, but by the early 1800s there were probably quite a few 'schools' in Froyle. These 'Dame Schools', as they were known, were small private ventures run by older women, who would charge about two pence a week for each pupil. A picture of such an institution is given in William Shenstone's often-quoted "The Schoolmistress". The poem dates from 1742, but there were schools in existence for more than another century of which the description would still hold good:

> *In ev'ry village mark'd with little spire*
> *Embow'r'd in trees and hardly known to fame,*
> *There dwells, in lowly shed, and mean attire,*
> *A matron old, whom we Schoolmistress name;*
> *Who boasts unruly brats with birch to tame;*
> *They grieven sore, in piteous durance pent,*

Nearly seventy years later the poet Crabbe describes a town dame school of much the same type:

> *Yet one there is, that small regard to rule*
> *Or study pays, and still is deemed a school;*
> *That where a deaf, poor, patient widow sits*
> *And awes some thirty infants as she knits-*
> *Infants of humble, busy wives, who pay*
> *Some trifling price for freedom through the day.*

It is obvious that, on the whole, dame schools were little more than baby minding establishments and that the education which they gave was extremely rudimentary.

However, in the Census of 1841 we see the first signs of real education in the village. Here is George Croucher, whose occupation is given as Schoolmaster. We were extremely fortunate, through the Froyle Archive web site, to receive an e-mail from a direct descendant, Daryl Cook, who lives in Port Carling, Canada. Daryl was not only able to tell us something about George Croucher, but she also provided us with this wonderful photograph of the man himself.

Daryl tells us, "In the 1851 census George Croucher is listed as a schoolmaster, age 47, living on Lower Street with five children. At this time they were living in a house in the north end of the village. His grandson, George William Croucher, recalls in his autobiography that the house was opposite Westbrook Farm which was his grandmother Sarah's home. George William was born in his grandparents' house in 1856. He remembers the large schoolroom in the house, although by 1856 his grandparents had moved to Crondall and classes were no longer taught there. Sometime between 1851 and 1856, following his time as schoolmaster in Froyle, George Croucher Sr. took a position as Superintendent of the District Schools at Wimble Hill, Crondall. He was fond of gardening and was an authority on flowers and bulbs and it is more than likely that he had a beautiful garden at his home and school in Froyle."

The photograph above, taken around 1938, shows what in George Croucher's time was known as Westbrook Farm. It was here that his wife, Sarah Westbrook's family lived. The Croucher's house and school was, according to his grandson, opposite, so we can imagine it standing where these cows graze. By the time this photograph was taken the house was long gone and Westbrook, or Rock House Farm, as it became known, would itself be demolished in the 1960s.

The censuses also tell us that there was another 'day school' in 1861, this time in Husseys Lane, Lower Froyle, in the cottage which is today Husseys Farmhouse. This school was run by thirty-nine year old Harriett Walker, whose father, James, was a General Dealer. Tradition tells us that there was also a school in Park Lane, Lower Froyle, and for many years this road was known as 'School House Lane'. But there is no evidence whatsoever that there was ever a school here, so perhaps this name arose from the fact that in the 1871 Census the lane was known as 'Croucher's Lane'. There was a Croucher living in the lane at this time, but it wasn't George, the schoolmaster, it was his brother, John, who was a carpenter. Could that have been how the confusion arose - who knows!

In 1857, soon after George Croucher left Froyle, Henry Burningham of Froyle House built a school room on to the front of one of his properties in Upper Froyle, now known as Froyle Cottage. This he did in memory of his young son, Francis Carleton Burningham, who had died in December 1856 at the age of seven. The school was run by twenty-one year old Letitia Enefer, the daughter of Henry Burningham's coachman.

The school was believed to have been held in the extension seen, in the photograph above, on the right of the main house. Some seventy children were taught in the cramped conditions of this small building!

And so to the 1860s. Whilst Europe introduced State Education, the British Government only managed to form a Department of Education which could give small grants to schools such as the National and British schools which had been already built by the Church of England and Non-conformist Churches. The Government could not agree whether state education would be a good thing - "it must be cheap, efficient, or both!" The Prince Consort had made it quite clear how he stood regarding educating the working class, when he said,

> "The working man's children are not only his offspring but they constitute part of his productive power and work with him for the staff of life. The daughters especially are the handmaids of the house, the assistants of the mother, the nurses of the younger children, the aged and the sick. To deprive the labouring family of their help would be almost to paralyse its domestic existence."

The Newcastle Commission, set up in 1861, was to look at all existing schools and report back "what measures would be necessary to provide a sound but cheap education for all classes of people". Evidence given to the Commission by Reverend James Fraser in 1861 gives us an idea of the Victorian interpretation of the word 'Education', at least as far as the working classes were concerned!

"I doubt whether it would be desirable, with a view to the real interests of the peasant boy, to keep him at school till he was 14 or 15 years of age. But it is not impossible. We must make up our minds to see the last of him at 10 or 11. It is quite possible to teach a child all that is necessary for him to possess by the time that he is 10 years old. He shall be able to spell correctly the words that he will ordinarily have to use; he shall read a common narrative - the paragraph in the newspaper that he cares to read - with sufficient ease to be a pleasure to himself and to convey information to listeners; if gone to live at a distance from home, he shall write his mother a letter that shall be both legible and intelligible; he knows enough of ciphering to make out, or test the correctness of, a common shop bill; if he hears talk of foreign countries he has some notions as to the part of the habitable globe in which they lie; he has acquaintance enough with the Holy Scriptures to follow the arguments of a plain sermon, and a recollection of the truths taught him in his catechism to know what are the duties required of him."

As a result of the commission's work, the Vice President of the Education Board, Robert Lowe, introduced a scheme of 'payments by results' whereby each child at any existing school could earn that school 4 shillings a year for satisfactory attendance with an additional 8 shillings if the pupil passed examinations in reading, writing and arithmetic. This encouraged the churches to consider building more schools and it was at this stage that Froyle School was planned. There were discussions between Winchester Diocese, the local church and Sir Charles Hayes Miller of Froyle Place.

The Miller family had come to Froyle in 1770, when Sir Thomas Miller, 5th Baronet, formerly of Lavant, near Chichester, purchased Froyle Place with the whole of the manorial rights. He was M.P. for Lewes from 1774 to 1778 and for Portsmouth from 1806 until his death in 1816. His son, the Reverend Sir Thomas Combe Miller, became vicar of Froyle in 1811 and on the death of his father, became Lord of the Manor. In turn, his son, Charles Hayes Miller, became the 7th Baronet on his father's death in 1864.

This photograph of Sir Charles was taken in 1867, around the time that the building of the new school was started. Local stone was used

Sir C.J.Hubert Miller seen on the left as a child of 9 and, right, on his 70th birthday

from nearby Quarry Bottom with Sir Charles Hayes' son, Charles John Hubert Miller, then a child of nine, laying the foundation stone of the new school on the 15th August 1867. It was an association that would remain dear to his heart throughout his life.

Tragically, halfway through the building operations, at the age of just 38, Sir Charles Hayes Miller died and this must surely have dampened enthusiasm for the school considerably.

Froyle Church of England Mixed National School opened its doors for the first time on Monday November 2nd 1868, and if, in the 118 years of its existence, education within the building changed considerably, the building itself looked much the same 'to the end', perhaps still the 'best looking school' in Hampshire, as claimed by its last Headteacher!

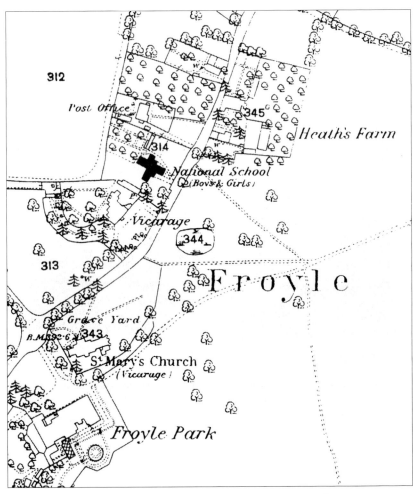

A map of 1870, showing the school, but surveyed
before the building of the schoolhouse in 1869.
The Miller residence, then known as Froyle Park,
can be seen adjacent to St Mary's Church

The Early Years

This is the earliest official group photograph of Froyle School, taken in 1882.
It shows Mr George Veal, the school's first Master, with his wife, pupils and dog!

The 'Edith' referred to in the margin is Edith Brownjohn. She was one of ten children
of Thomas and Caroline Brownjohn, who ran the village stores in Lower Froyle

FROYLE Church of England Mixed National School officially opened on the afternoon of Monday, November 2nd, 1868. Following a Service in St Mary's Church, Upper Froyle, everyone walked down the road to the new school, where the opening ceremony was performed by the Vicar, the Reverend W.R.Astley-Cooper. No doubt, had Sir Charles Hayes Miller still been alive, he would have been asked to undertake this duty, so the opening would have been tinged with sadness and the Vicar surely must have made reference to the generosity of Sir Charles.

Mr George Veal had been appointed 'Master' of the new school and he was assisted by his wife and three monitors. Thirty four children had already been registered by their parents on the previous Saturday - perhaps this was because they could not attend the opening on November 2nd, we do not know - and one hundred and four were registered on the first day of school. Of these, twenty two had come from various Dame Schools in and around the village and seventy three had transferred from Mrs Burningham's school just up the road. Most of the families lived in Upper or Lower Froyle but some also came from Yarnhams, Sutton Common, Coldrey, Mill Court and Isington as shown on the map below.

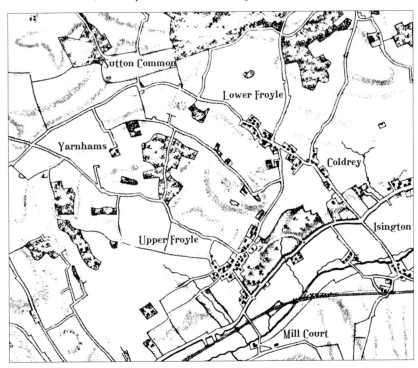

Their parents were employed locally, about half as labourers on the land, while one or two were bailiffs for local farmers. Other parents worked as servants at the big houses, ranging from butlers and head gardeners to coachmen, woodmen and gamekeepers. The remaining parents worked in the village as innkeepers, shopkeepers, carpenters, bakers, shoemakers, bricklayers, blacksmiths, with at least one drayman, one carrier and a 'grinder'. Children of small farmers also attended the school, but those of the local gentry were catered for privately, although they were sometimes brought on a visit to the school.

For a complete list of the admissions, turn to the Appendix, page 193.

At the end of the day Mr Veal wrote the first of many entries he would make in the school log book,

"The schools in this village were formally opened today. There was afternoon service in the Church, the vicar of Alton was the preacher; after service the children and their parents assembled in the school rooms, when the schools were opened by the vicar of the parish, afterwards the children were regaled with cake and tea which had been provided for them in commemoration of the event."

(Monday, November 2ⁿᵈ 1868)

These school log books are invaluable to the local historian, as they describe the day to day running of the school. Those belonging to Froyle School are intact, which means that we know exactly what went on in the school from the day it opened until the day it closed in 1986. The amount of information contained within its pages depended very much on the Headteacher of the time. In some cases the entries amounted to one line a week, while in others, as in the case of the school's last Headteacher, Mrs Nora Jupe, every single day was described in great detail. Mrs Jupe, a historian herself, appreciated the importance of recording as much as she could. But, tantalisingly, while the entries give us the essential facts, they do not contain comments or opinions and so we are often left to imagine for ourselves what lies behind some of the entries. The entry for November 2ⁿᵈ 1868 really tells us nothing about the atmosphere of that first day. It would have been a most auspicious one for the whole village and very overwhelming for the children, although the cake and tea would certainly have been a real treat. The schoolrooms themselves must have seemed palatial compared with the cramped conditions in which the children had previously been taught. Everything was so new and different, not only for the children, but also for the parents, many of whom had themselves received no education whatsoever and would have been unable to even sign their name.

Before going any further, let's take a general look at what education was like in those early days. As we have already seen, the government's revised code of education in 1862 had established a system known as "payment by results", so great attention was paid to attendance figures for many years, as Department of Education grants were partly dependent on the numbers on roll and the average attendances. Schools that sought funding were visited by a government inspector (H.M.I.) every autumn. This was a great ordeal for both children and teachers. Children who passed the inspector's examination moved up to a higher standard - and the size of the school's grant, as well as the teacher's salary, depended on the number of children who passed. Very little was taught except reading, writing, and arithmetic. The church societies required that a clergyman come into school regularly for religious instruction, but teachers had almost no motivation to spend time on history, geography, science, or practical subjects.

The school fee was 3d a week, and schooling was not to be free for another twenty years or more. This money was to be brought on Monday mornings and if forgotten, the children were sent home for it - this meant that some of them did not come back for the rest of the week! Kind employers sometimes paid the school fees for their employees' children, particularly any arrears, but the girls could be exempt by turning up each Saturday morning to scrub and clean the schoolrooms. Many parents would struggle to provide the necessary 3d, rather than be thought of as poor,

"Some of the girls parents objected to scrubbing the room, a new regulation has been made for the future that they pay 3d a week and be exempt." *(December 22nd 1868)*

And it wasn't long before other arrangements had to be made to keep the school clean.

"An arrangement has been made today that a woman should be employed every Saturday to teach the elder girls to clean the room properly; two girls are expected to come every Saturday instead of six as was arranged at first, as most of the elder girls pay threepence per week to be exempt from cleaning." *(October 1869)*

There were six 'Standards' whereby a child could climb the ladder of learning at this time. To give you an idea of just what was expected of them, here is "The Revised Code of 1862: Standards of Achievement" as published in a Parliamentary Paper of that year:-

Standard I

Reading: Narrative in monosyllables.

Writing: Form on blackboard or slate, from dictation, letters, capital and small manuscript.

Arithmetic: Form on blackboard or slate, from dictation, figures up to 20; name at sight figures up to 20; add and subtract figures up to 10, orally, from examples on blackboard.

Standard II
> Reading: One of the narratives next in order after monosyllables in an elementary reading book used in the school.
> Writing: Copy in manuscript character a line of print.
> Arithmetic: A sum in simple addition or subtraction, and the multiplication table.

Standard III
> Reading: A short paragraph from an elementary reading book used in the school.
> Writing: A sentence from the same paragraph, slowly read once, and then dictated in single words.
> Arithmetic: A sum in any simple rule as far as short division (inclusive).

Standard IV
> Reading: A short paragraph from a more advanced reading book used in the school.
> Writing: A sentence slowly dictated once by a few words at a time from the same book, but not from the paragraph read.
> Arithmetic: A sum in compound rules (money).

Standard V
> Reading: A few lines of poetry from a reading book used in the first class of the school.
> Writing: A sentence slowly dictated once, by a few words at a time, from a reading book used in the first class of the school.
> Arithmetic: A sum in compound rules (common weights and measures).

Standard VI
> Reading: A short ordinary paragraph in a newspaper, or other modern narrative.
> Writing: Another short ordinary paragraph in a newspaper, or other modern narrative, slowly dictated once a few words at a time.
> Arithmetic: A sum in practice bills of parcels.

And what was a typical school day like in 1868? Here is a very detailed example, and although this is a generalisation, it is more than likely how Froyle children were taught.

8.50 Entrance Drill - The bell is rung. Children line up, boys and girls separate, in height order. They begin marching on spot on order 'left, right'. On the order 'Enter' boys lead in first, girls follow, filing in and standing in the aisle by their desks – in silence. Boys with hands behind backs. Girls with hands clasped in front. The teacher then greets the children 'Good morning'. The children respond, saying 'Good morning Sir'. The boys will bow and the girls curtsy. On the command 'In' the children step in front of their chairs.

9.00 Registration - The Master calls the names on the register. Each child bows or curtsies and answers 'Sir'. He inspects nails, shoes and girls hair length, then questions last weeks absentees and friends of today's absentees. A lecture follows on punctuality with reference to future employment and the use of the cane if unpunctuality occurs again is threatened.

9.20 Scripture - The time is spend committing Bible verses to memory, often with the Vicar.

9.50 The Text - The lesson this morning is 'To order myself lowly and reverently before my betters. Your betters are the landowners, the Squire, the Vicar and all who provide employment for you. You come to school to prepare yourself for future work. What you learn here you apply to working life. Repeat after me.

I must not lie or steal.
I must not be discontented or envious.
God has placed me where I am in the social order.
He has given me my work to do.
I must not envy others.
I will not try to change my lot in life.
It is a sin of which I will never be guilty.'

10.00 Arithmetic - Drill-like manner, using cane to maintain the pace of speaking.

10.15 Play-time - Children to play with hoops and skipping ropes.

10.30 Writing - Monitors collect spelling books and hand out writing scripts, slates, and chalk. The Master shows children examples of copperplate writing. He reminds children that the script must slope at an angle of 60 degrees. Upward strokes are light and downward strokes are heavier. He emphasises the importance of good handwriting for any child wishing to become a clerk. 'Good children try not to blot their copy books'. Chalk up! Chalk down. Begin. Children should work in silence, without looking at each others work. When finished – 'Chalk up! Chalk on desks.

11.00 Drill - This is undertaken outside, unless the weather is really inclement

11.45 Reading - Monitors hand out reading scripts. 'Eyes front. Hands palms on desk. We shall as usual read around the class. I shall punish children who lose their places.' The Master taps time to keep pace. Individual readings, followed by class reading in unison.

12.15 Prayers & Closing School Session - The class all rise and repeat:-

Thank you for the world so sweet, Thank you for the food we eat,
Thank you for the birds that sing, Thank you God for everything. Amen.

The Master says, 'Good morning children. 'Step into the aisle. March – left/right, left/right. Class dismiss.' The children march out row by row.

Most children go home for lunch. How pleased they must be to be away from the disciplined regime. But it doesn't last long.

1.30 Children line up and enter.

1.35 'Good afternoon children'. Registration. Shoes and hand inspection.

1.45 Spelling - Monitors hand out the spelling books. The class sit up straight, hands palms down on desks and repeat the alphabet in unison, keeping in time.

2.15 Needlework & Drawing

3.00 Play time

3.15 Singing & Poetry

3.50 Prayers & Closing of School

4.00 Pupil Teachers Lessons - Intelligent boys and girls were encouraged to stay at school by offering them positions as monitors. After turning thirteen years old they could be hired as pupil teachers, although the pay was barely enough for clothes and spending money; they had to come from families that could afford for them to continue living at home without contributing to the family income. This Parliamentary Paper of 1847 sets out the necessary criteria:

Pupil Teachers: Qualification of Candidates

1. They must be at least thirteen years of age, and must not be subject to any bodily infirmity likely to impair their usefulness as pupil teachers. Candidates will also be required,
2. To read with fluency, ease, and expression.
3. To write in a neat hand, with correct spelling and punctuation, a simple prose narrative slowly read to them.
4. To write from dictation sums in the first four rules of arithmetic, simple and compound; to work them correctly, and to know the tables of weights and measures.
5. To point out the parts of speech in a simple sentence.
6. To have an elementary knowledge of geography.
7. *In schools connected with the Church of England,* they will be required to repeat the Catechism, and to show that they understand its meaning, and are acquainted with the outline of Scripture history. The parochial clergyman will assist in this part of the examination. *In other schools* the state of the religious knowledge will be certified by the managers.
8. To teach a junior class to the satisfaction of the Inspector.
9. Girls should also be able to sew neatly and to knit.

In addition to helping in the classroom, pupil teachers received evening lessons in secondary-school subjects from the headteacher. When they reached eighteen, they could pass an examination called 'The Queen's Scholarship' and attend training college to earn a teaching certificate.

This set of Victorian School Rules gives some idea of how strict discipline could be:-

1. Children must stand up to answer questions and wait to be given permission to speak.
2. Children must call teachers 'Sir' or 'Miss'.
3. Children must stand when an adult enters the room.
4. Children must wear clean shoes and clothes.
5. Children must sit and stand with straight backs.
6. Children must use the right hand at all times for writing.
7. Girls must wear their hair tied back with string or plain ribbons.
8. Girls will learn needlework and boys will learn drawing.
9. The children will line up, boys and girls separately, with the smallest in front and the tallest at the back.
10. Prizes will be given for good attendance.
11. Children must not speak unless spoken to.
12. Children must not put their hand up unless told they can do.
13. Children must not ask questions.
14. Children who truant, are late, behave badly or do poor work will be caned.
15. Talking and fidgeting will be punished.
16. Counting on fingers is forbidden.
17. Children with fleas, nits or contagious diseases should not attend school.

Now that we have an idea of how the Victorian school was run, let's return to Froyle!

Mr George Leith Veal was only 27 when he took on the job of Master. He was born in Poole, Dorset, and was a certificated teacher. We do not know where he and his wife Jane, who was also 27, were living to begin with, as the schoolhouse adjacent to the school was not built until at least 1869. By the Census of 1871, however, they were residing at the "Village School House".

During those first four years in Froyle the Veals had to deal with personal tragedy, suffering the loss of both their young daughters. In April 1870 their second born, Eveline, died at the age of just six weeks. Just over nine months later their first born, Helen Leith Veal, died in January 1871, at the age of 3 years old. She had been a babe in arms when the Veals moved to Froyle. This double tragedy is something that today, we would find hard to recover from, but one should remember that, in Victorian times, deaths of babies and children were a common fact of life which afflicted all classes, though to varying degrees. Deaths in the first year of life were chiefly attributed to diarrhoea, pneumonia, bronchitis, and convulsions, while measles and whooping-cough became more lethal in the second year. Scarlet fever had its most fatal impact between the ages of two and five. The major reason for the decline in the infant and child mortality rate in the Edwardian period was the dramatic reduction in deaths from infectious diseases, which mainly affected the young. The Veals had two more children who survived, at least beyond childhood. George Leith junior was born in 1873, and Archibald James in 1880.

Naturally, these details of the Veals personal life were not gleaned from the school log books, but from the village's church records. Over the period of both losses, life appeared to carry on as usual at school, with not a hint of tragedy nor any record of Mrs Veal taking time off for the birth of any of her children. However, in the Census of 1881, we see that the Veals had a domestic servant, thirteen year old Kate Burningham, who lived in. Possibly she took care of young Archibald while his mother was teaching next door.

Jane Veal had been unqualified when she came to Froyle but finally obtained her teacher's certificate and was able to be paid in her own right instead of sharing her husband's salary of £110 per annum. A second certificated teacher was not required unless numbers rose above 200 on roll. Monitors at this time included thirteen year old Clara Baker and eleven year old Anne Kemp, who were employed at a salary of 9d a week.

Froyle School around 1900

On Tuesday, 3rd November, 1868, the first full school day commenced. George Veal noted in the log book that Mrs Veal had taken Needlework in the afternoon and had also instructed the Infants and Standard I in the morning. The very next day he had his first real problem with discipline, when one youngster decided that the only way to settle an argument was with his teeth!

"James Rampton corrected today for having bit another boy in the arm."   *(November 4th 1868)*

We do not know how this 'correction' was carried out, but one would imagine it was by the use of the cane. One hundred and fifteen years later James Rampton's grandson, Howard, visited the school with his wife, while on a trip to England from their home in Australia. They were fascinated to be shown the entry in the log book and asked if they could photograph it to convince their family back home that they had found their Froyle ancestor, even if, as Howard laughingly remarked afterwards, "he appears to have been a cannibal!"

With no village hall in Froyle at this time, the new school building became the hub of the community. The Parish Council held its meetings there in the evening, many social events were held there and, when necessary, the children were sent home early if the building was needed for something more important! Just two days after it opened we read in the log book:-

"The children were dismissed at 11.45 this morning as the people belonging to the clothing club were coming to show their things."
(November 5th 1868)

On Tuesday, 10th November, Lady Miller, the widow of Sir Charles Hayes, the benefactor of the school, paid a visit to see how everyone was settling in. She was accompanied by Mrs Burningham, who, the following year, would donate all the books from her small school. Local gentry visited on a regular basis, often bringing any family or friends who were staying with them. Occasionally they gave presents to the school, which for many years was short of stock. Mr Hardy, a local landowner and school manager, visited the school in February 1869 with an offer of help for the Headmaster :-

"Mr Hardy came in this afternoon and promised to give each boy in the school a pinafore and belt, and also to pay a man to cut the boys' hair once a month."

Mr Hardy and his family lived at Froyle Place in Upper Froyle and sadly, by the Census of 1871, he had passed away, so we do not really know for how long the children received their pinafores and belts and had their hair cut. These gifts were, no doubt, intended to improve the boys' tidiness and cleanliness; the girls mostly wore white frilled aprons over their dresses and had their hair tied back. Their aprons must have meant hard work for their mothers, washing them in a tub and ironing them with a flat iron! Mr Hardy also provided a Christmas Tree treat that year for the children in school and both the Hardy and Burningham families gave a treat on the occasion of their own children's weddings. Books and pictures were presented to the school and generally the wealthier members of the community supported it. They did however expect the children to behave properly and treat them with respect with the customary tugging of forelocks and curtsying. Most parents accepted this and themselves respected the school staff and managers; a few parents sometimes rebelled or complained but usually apologised fairly quickly as they did not wish to be frowned on by members of the village community.

Attendance at first was not that good, something which would have been of concern to the Veals, since the grants they received depended a great deal on the attendance of the children. There were, however, many reasons for staying away, especially during exceptionally wet weather. With no real waterproof clothing available, children would set out on the long walk to school on a wintry morning, and arrive drenched to the skin. The only means of drying out clothes at school was an open fire in each classroom. The teachers were responsible for stoking the fireplaces during the day but often there was a shortage of fuel. If the children got wet going home at dinner time, they often did not return in the afternoon. Most of them walked home for their dinners although the distant ones probably brought bread and cheese and they might even have been allowed to make a mug of cocoa in the winter.

"The severity of the weather still keeps the numbers low, many are away with colds and bad feet."   *(January 10ᵗʰ 1871)*

Boots and shoes were expensive to buy and had to last a long time, being passed down to younger members of the family. Some children went barefoot, particularly in the towns. There was a shoemaker in the village but most cottages had a 'shoe-last' on which to mend the family's shoes, a task often undertaken by the mothers! Boots and shoes would wear out quickly on the rough roads and lanes of Froyle and leaking footwear would soon saturate the thick hand-knitted socks. There were many foot ailments in those days, including chilblains in the winter months.

One of the main causes of absenteeism was that of children helping their parents on the land or in their homes.

"Kate Adams and Jane Smith given leave of absence to help their mother and because of the death of their grandfather.
(November 16ᵗʰ 1868)

Ellen Mayhew has asked leave for the whole of the week to assist her mother.   *(December 13ᵗʰ 1870)*

Until the coming of compulsory education children worked alongside their parents in the fields, almost as soon as they could walk. So, when they had to go to school they were still expected to put in their share of agricultural work during the busiest times of the year. Absenteeism coincided with the different growing seasons. In May the children would be needed for hop tying, while in June there would be hop clearing and haymaking.

"The attendance of elder children not at all good. Haymaking is about commencing. The irregularity interferes much with a uniform system of working... I fear there are many children who will not put in an appearance until after the Harvest Holiday ... Parents are very much disposed to take children with them into the fields instead of sending them to school ..." (June 1877)

"Now the hops are nearly done the children are wanted for haymaking and as soon as that is finished for harvest... The children were so tired on Wednesday that several went to sleep....." (June 24th 1877)

July's afternoon timetable had to be rescheduled so that the children could take tea to their fathers working in the fields and it would seem that the poor teachers often used to have to rely on our old friend the British weather to help them out!

"There was a better attendance this week as the rain has put a stop to out door work for a short time..." (July 1877)

Then along came August, the busiest month, when the harvesting was the main occupation. There was no point keeping children at school during this busy time, especially in rural communities, and so the long Summer, or Harvest Holiday, as it was known, came into being. It was usually five or six weeks and was timed, often at short notice and by the managers consent, to fit in with the corn and hop harvests. It was usually the second half of August and the whole of September and it lasted longer some years than others.

"The school closed... and will not meet again until the harvest and hop picking is over which will be about six weeks from this time if the weather be favourable!" (August 22nd 1872)

"..... as hop picking was not finished at the end of the six weeks the managers agreed to give another week." (October 7th 1872)

Even when school began again in October there was still pole stripping and acorn picking to keep the youngsters away from their studies. In most cases parents made their children work in the fields, rather than in the schoolroom, through necessity. Without the extra money they brought in there was just insufficient to go round. So the youngsters found themselves doing the jobs of men and women during the school holidays. No wonder they were so worn out when they went back to school.

They had often become very rough during the Harvest Holidays and Mr Veal and Masters after him complained of this in the log books. The boys, in particular, used bad language and bullied younger children in the playground. On several occasions they were accused of upsetting the girls on their way to and from school and had to stay behind to give the girls time to get out of their way. They sometimes played truant in Froyle Park; they tripped children up in the playground, or hit them with sticks. They climbed stack pipes:-

William Chitty was hung by his arm to one of the stack pipes after school, in attempting to get a bird's nest; and we had great trouble to extricate him."   *(May 20th 1872)*

They were accused of throwing stones at the school bell, stopping it from ringing. Reverend Astley-Cooper, who was a school manager,
"... came in and assisted to make investigations." Benjamin Cains, Alfred Feltham and William Taylor were found to be the culprits on this occasion. Mr Veal wrote in his log book that,

"It was hoped the bell wasn't injured."   *(December 15th 1874)*

They stole school pence and garden produce from nearby cottages during the dinner hour. In school they were inattentive, ate walnuts, spilt ink, lost keys; once they even broke the blackboard and easel. Wandering families, gypsies and travellers, often caused most bother, as they did not feel part of the village community and their children were often undisciplined and backward.

These three entries from Mr Veal's log book gives you some idea of the sort of punishment metered out to the perpetrators.

"William Blunden was caned this morning for refusing to read to his teacher."   *(December 1869)*

"James Haddick was a very idle boy. Locked him in the woodhouse in his play hour."   *(April 1870)*

"George Giles, Frank Stevens, Walter Brownjohn were very inattentive at the singing lessons. They were detained for half an hour and given a lesson to write on slates."   *(July 1872)*

And so continued the daily routine of school. English and Arithmetic took the main part of every morning with a little drill or physical exercise, done in straight lines in the playground (weather permitting and if not too muddy!) The Vicar sometimes took Religious Instruction at the beginning of the morning, otherwise it was taken by Mr Veal. The girls were expected to do Needlework every afternoon, taken by Mrs Veal, while the Infants were supervised by the pupil-teachers. Anne Kemp, who had been a Monitor when the school opened in 1868, was joined by George Clements and Minnie Chitty.

This Bible, now in the Froyle Archive, actually belonged to Minnie Chitty. A label inside the front cover, dated December 2nd 1876, records the fact that it was awarded to 'Minnie Chitty, pupil teacher at Froyle School, for excellence in Religious Knowledge'. The Froyle Archive acquired the Bible in the summer of 2001 when we received a phone call from a Miss Yates who told us that she still had her grandmother's bible and, as she had no descendants, wanted it to 'go back home'. So how did it pass into the Yates family? A quick check of the Church Records for St Mary's reveals that on October 20th 1885 Francis Minnie Chitty had married one Philip Thomas Yates at Froyle Church - hence the connection. Minnie was 18 years old at the time she received the prize and her grand-daughter told us that she went on to become a fully qualified teacher.

The Chitty family - her parents were Henry and Elizabeth - are shown in the 1871 Census as living in Upper Froyle, somewhere between Blundens and the Church. Henry was a gardener and the family had moved to Froyle from the Frensham area. Minne is recorded in the Census as being born in Frensham, her two younger sisters, Constance and Olive, being born in Binsted and Froyle respectively. By 1891 Henry and Elizabeth had moved to Mill Court Cottages, Minnie and Constance had married and left Froyle. The Froyle Archive is honoured to have received such a gift with connections with the Froyle of so long ago.

Back to 1875! The boys carried on with ordinary work with the Master. There was an hour's music lesson each week, given by a visitor, Miss Simpson. The Junior children were entered for examinations in Reading, Writing and Arithmetic each year. A few children were not entered as there was no hope of them passing, or earning the school extra money, of course! Each year an Education Inspector visited the school and his report was sent back to the managers and then filed in school in a locked portfolio. Each year the school's report was satisfactory, often very good, but nearly always Arithmetic was the weakest subject. The children were usually commended for their singing. Lists of songs for the year were written out in the log book; how the boys must have enjoyed songs such as 'Hurrah for England' or 'Jack Frost',but the girls probably preferred 'The Violet' or 'The Pet Lamb'!

Occasionally sudden emergencies arose, such as a counting bead stuck in a child's nose, a penny being swallowed - old pennies were a lot larger than the present 1p! Injuries were caused by falling, or being pushed over, on the rough playground surface. At this time the playground would have been hard earth, not gravelled or tarmac-surfaced as in later years, the girls and infants were separated from the boys by a fence, however! An ulcerated leg kept one child away from school for some months, consumption (T.B.) finished one child's schooling completely as it was infectious and usually fatal.

Several children's deaths are recorded in the first few years of the school's logs. One child was burnt to death in a cottage fire; the whole village lined the road from the school to the Church for some of these funerals. Public health had improved tremendously in the nineteenth century but there were still many infectious diseases and very little vaccination. These infections spread rapidly and the children of whole families were excluded from school at first to prevent an epidemic from spreading.

> *"Kate Adams is ill with fever, the other children are to stay at home until she is better, according to the Rules of the School."*
>
> *(February 24th 1869)*

> *"After School work was over the School was closed until further notice on account of the spread of measles in the Parish, under medical authority, the following letter having been received by the Vicar:-*
> *Dear Sir, I have in Lower Froyle between 20 & 30 cases of measles. Under the circumstances I think it highly desirous that the School should be closed for 2 or 3 weeks. Faithfully yours, Walter Sheppard."*
>
> *(December 29th 1870)*

Check out the date of this log entry! No long holidays for children in those days! They were given Christmas Day and Good Friday off, but were always back at school on Boxing Day and Easter Monday! Where closures such as the one above were enforced, the children were given extra instruction when they eventually returned to school, with classes continuing until 5pm every day until the lost work had been made up! Even so, closure of the school owing to epidemics not only made it very difficult to complete the compulsory number of attendance to qualify for grants but also effected its performance. The H.M.I.'s Inspection in February 1871 points out,

> *"The School has suffered much from a recent epidemic, but, circumstances considered, its condition both as regards order and attainments is creditable to its Teachers."*

The Inspectors annually declared the discipline in school 'quite satisfactory' or in 'good order', except on one occasion towards the end of Mr Veal's career.

This group of 1882 features Alfred Brownjohn, the brother of Edith
who we met on page 11. In later life he would carry on his father's
grocer's business alongside his brother Walter

In 1883 Alfred, seen here second row, far left, moved on to
Eggars Grammar School in the nearby town of Alton

In the summer of 1884, after nearly twenty years as Master, with its trials and tribulations, George Veal and his wife left Froyle School. The log book entry for Monday October 6th, 1884 suddenly records,

"We, John and Isabella Perry, commenced duties in the school today, reopening the school after eight weeks holiday."

It recorded no mention of Mr and Mrs Veal leaving or where they went, or the hustle and bustle of moving in and out of the schoolhouse next door, or the re-organising of the school buildings and equipment which must have taken place during those two month's holiday. The Education Codes had now been revised; more money was available, priorities were changing, drawing as well as needlework was important, there was even talk of woodwork and metalwork! The new Master must have had much to think about; the last Inspector's report had commented that,

"...there was hesitation in awarding the merit grant that year, due both to scholars' behaviour and also arithmetic results."

There was always the worry of keeping up attendances to ensure as much grant money as possible. However, both Mr Perry and his wife were certificated teachers and Miss Simpson joined the staff as a full-time assistant. More mention was now made of musical drill and singing; stock was handed over by the Vicar, not only maps, pictures and books, but also a new blackboard and easel, a handbell, and a coal scuttle and shovels.

Kindergarten lessons were a new venture in the Infants Class, and the Master frequently stressed the need for good behaviour. Stone throwing, stealing and truancy still continued - the seventeen boys who disappeared in Froyle Park one playtime must have regretted it later, when they lost their playtime for the rest of the week. Attendance did not improve greatly in spite of attendance officers' visits and the issue of 'free tickets' each month by the Vicar for perfect attendance the previous month. However, the Diocesan Inspector was well pleased with the school when he made his report in February, 1886.

"The results of the examination are very satisfactory - the children appear to be intelligent and interested in their work; and the considerable percentage in each class answering correctly is evidence of patient and careful teaching. The written exercises were very fairly done. The elder scholars are quite capable of further instruction in portions of the Prayer Book. The Infants also passed a good examination, their repetition being remarkably good. The tone and discipline appear to be excellent throughout the school."

By the time of Queen Victoria's Golden Jubilee in June 1887, things were getting better and the future looked brighter for both teachers and children.

Enjoying the snow after school in Froyle Park in 1888

Mr Perry's log book entry of January 14th 1889 describes a busy school,

"*Read the notice of Diocesan Inspection and affix such notice in the school. The Religious examination will take place on Feb.5th next. Infants' Object Lesson for 1889. Hop-picking, Slate, Tea, Cow, A table, Windows, Potato, Form, Colour, Spring, Summer, Autumn, Winter, Sheep, Birds-nests, Fishes, Paper, Coal, Hen, Tiger, Cork, Duck, Cotton, Ostrich, Lion, Sugar, Coffee, Camel. List of Songs: Come in you naughty bird, The Cobbler, I'm a busy little Mother.*"

The last decade of the nineteenth century showed a settled school, growing in numbers and progressing steadily. 'The New Code' of 1890 finished payment by results in favour of a single grant, for ages 5 to 13, of between 12/6 and 14/- based solely on attendance.

The year 1891 saw the final end of school pence, with 10/- per annum per child paid to those schools which abolished fees. The money was government funded through the Department of Education, who made sure that all rules were adhered to at all times.

"*To the Rev H C Floud, Froyle Vicarage. 21st February, 1891*

Rev.Sir,

My Lords observe that the School has not been open 400 times during the past school year as required by Article 83. I am accordingly to request that you will send up a certificate, signed by the Local Sanitary Authority, in support of the closing of the School during part of the

28

last school year in consequence of epidemic sickness, and will give the exact dates of the period during which the School was closed. I have the honour to be, Rev.Sir, Your obedient Servant..."

Two years later a few special provisions were made nationally for some blind and deaf children and also for evening classes for adult education. Some villages had a 'Reading Room' for this, but schools were often used. The curriculum was widened, the boys now took Drawing three afternoons each week, whilst the girls continued with Needlework. The drawings were examined annually by an outside inspector but the needlework was checked only by the ladies of the village.

Elementary science and more physical exercises and games were encouraged; wooden dumb-bells came into use in drill during this period. Lists of Object Lessons for the Infants for the year were entered into the log book, and History, Geography and Nature Study were important Junior subjects. In 1891 however, the log book records the Master and his wife attending an interview by the Caterham School Board and as a result of their promotion, the entry for April 6th 1891 reads,

"Commenced duty as Master and Mistress of these schools today."

It was written by Arthur Mann, whose wife Elizabeth was already a certificated teacher. The managers agreed that the new Master and his wife should be paid £110.00 a year, by quarterly payments on the first day of January, April, July and October. They were also given the use of the Schoolhouse and premises during the term of their engagement, along with fuel - wood and coal - to a 'reasonable amount'.

The Manns were assisted by two pupil teachers, Annie Cunningham and Florence Robinson, but there is now no mention of Miss Simpson on the staff. Florence Robinson was the fourteen year old daughter of Thomas Robinson, who was both a carpenter by trade and the Froyle Postmaster, and the family lived at the Post Office in Upper Froyle. Florence had been engaged as a Pupil Teacher on January 1st 1891 and her Agreement, which was for a period of three years, states that,

"The managers shall pay to the pupil-teacher as wages eight pounds in the first year, and this sum shall be increased two pounds in each subsequent year of the engagement: but such increase may be stopped at the discretion of the managers of the said school for the time being for the unexpired remainder of any year after receipt of notice from the Education Department that the Pupil Teacher has failed to pass her examination and to fulfill the other conditions of the Pupil Teacher according to the standard of the preceding year as prescribed in the articles of the Code."

The Mann's stay was to be a short one of only five terms and they were difficult ones. The pupils' standard of work was criticised and the Inspector commented that,

"Instruction had been affected by changes of teacher and much illness in the village."

During that short time however, Mr Mann managed to make a few changes. A Penny Savings Bank was started, as well as an Adult Cookery Class, which was held in the Infant room on Thursday afternoons, a new cooking range having been installed there. This was not entirely satisfactory as the Infants had to be divided up in the other two classrooms each Thursday, which inevitably affected the work of the whole school; also for the remainder of the week,

"the stove emitted a strong smell of sulphur which at times is almost unbearable."

The cookery lessons seem to have ended rather abruptly, but for years to come there were to be problems and constant criticisms of the heating of the Infant room!

Without any prior warning, the log book entry for December 19th 1892 recorded,

"Took charge of these schools,", signed, *"William Downes."*

As this was not quite at the end of the school term, did this take scholars and their parents by surprise? We shall never know why the Manns left, but they were replaced by a young couple who were to shape the future of Froyle School for the next thirty years.

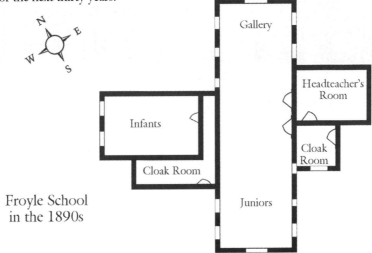

Froyle School
in the 1890s

Suffer Little Children

Mr Downes, his wife Alice, and their four children (centre)
pose with a school group in 1900

Willam Button Downes was thirty years old when he took up his post as Master of Froyle Church of England Mixed School in the December of 1892. We believe, from our research, that he trained as a teacher at St Peter's Training College of Schoolmasters in Peterborough. He moved into the Froyle schoolhouse with his wife, Alice Lucy, who was just twenty-two. The Downes stay was to be a long one - they did not leave the school until 1922, thirty years later. They raised four children in Froyle; Dorothy Mabel, born in 1895, Margaret Vera, 1897; Herbert Frederick, 1898; and Ruth Ellen Mary, 1899. The children attended the school, moving on to Eggars School in Alton when they were older. They helped out with the teaching at Froyle on many occasions, so the running of the school was a real family affair. In 1892 Mr Downes taught the older children, while his wife, who was uncertificated at that time, taught the Infants as well as Needlework. They appointed another pupil teacher, fifteen year old Lilian Coster, whose father, Harry, was the Head Gardener at Froyle Place. Mr Coster became a school manager and, in 1897, was elected Chairman of Froyle Parish Council. Some time later the Master's sister Emma also joined the staff.

For the first time the taking of school photographs was actually recorded in the log book, with groups being taken on 29th March 1893.

Note the sombre colours the children are all wearing, apart from the two little girls in the second row, who are in very patterned clothing for that period. Several of the boys are wearing celluloid collars, which look as uncomfortable as they really were. The lady teachers didn't fare much better, so tightly laced into their corsets they could hardly breathe! School photographs were usually taken outside the front porch, a tradition that continued until the school closed in 1986, and at first, they were at five yearly intervals. This ensured that each child was photographed at least once during his or her school career, but it was expensive for the parents, many of whom could not afford copies.

Payment of grants according to school attendances meant that the Master was continually preoccupied with registers and absences, as is obvious from log book entries. It was a great offence to mark a register incorrectly and the alteration had to be clearly entered and initialled by the headteacher. Erasures were forbidden and the managers periodically checked the register entries and totals and recorded this in the log book.

Extreme weather did not help attendance. There were at least two hurricanes, violent thunderstorms, torrential rain causing flooding - occasionally even inside the school; there was icy weather with heavy snowfalls, mist and fog, but also the summers were extremely hot, very often turning to thundery rain at harvest time. The school floors must have been the despair of the caretaker at times, and the smell of damp woollen clothing must have often pervaded the atmosphere. Conditions for drying off clothes in the children's homes were little, if any, better than those at school so it was not surprising that parents did not send their children on very wet mornings, or return them for the afternoon session if they got wet at dinner time.

There were many necessary absences for infectious diseases, these included measles, mumps, chicken pox, whooping cough, scarlet fever, and, later, diphtheria. There were also skin infections such as scabies, ringworm and impetigo and children infected with head or body lice were also excluded. Under these circumstances, attendance figures appear remarkably good - often over 90% - but parents usually preferred their children to be at school as there were always younger ones still at home. In 1893 the school was closed from July until December by the local Sanitary Authority because of scarlet fever, which again flared up the following spring, so it was impossible to accumulate the necessary attendance figures. Over that period, however, the grant was still awarded, due to 'exceptional circumstances'. From 1894 onwards, Medical Officers of Health were appointed who took on the responsibility of advising the schools on health matters, but it was over ten years later before organised school health services were provided. The school was closed because of measles in 1895 and later for whooping cough, but in this way serious epidemics were prevented from spreading before the general advent of vaccination and immunisation.

Other absences were very much frowned on, such as children staying away to help in the home or helping parents who worked on local farms and estates.

Mr Charles Wood, a conscientious school manager, gave every child in the school an orange when the attendance reached 150 one week. This conflicted, however, with his letter to the headmaster, dated 18th December 1893, stating that schoolboys were necessary for 'beating' or 'stopping' at his shooting parties and this put the onus on the Master to forbid younger boys to stay away from school for the purpose.

> *"That great obstacle to all successful winter work in this school, 'beating', has affected us today. Eight boys are employed by Mr Wood of Froyle Park, among them being the son of one of the managers."*

The attraction of payment for such duties was so great for both parents and children that it was left to School Attendance Committees and their Officers to ensure compulsory attendance. Sometimes the Master sent a telegram to the Attendance Officer so that he could 'catch the offenders in the act' and, if necessary, take parents to court.

> *"19 boys away 'beating' for Mr Wood and Capt. Reid. Wrote to the Vicar about it. Mr Blackmore, Attendance Officer, called this afternoon taking away with him a full list of 'beaters' with names of the employers."*   *(December 1893)*

The school premises were gradually improved and better equipped and in November 1894 new lights were installed with duplex hanging burners and with large enamel shields to protect the ceilings from heat. These lamps were the property of the managers. Before this, Art and Needlework often had to be brought forward to the beginning of the afternoon on dark days and the children sang when it became too dark to see properly. Under Article 84B of the Revised Education Code, Inspectors were instructed to visit schools twice yearly, one to be a surprise visit, apart from the annual examinations visit. They could suggest or virtually order the managers to make certain improvements and, as a result, during the 1890s, new school desks were fitted and infant or 'kindergarten' desks were supplied. Lighting was improved by glass panelled doors and by tree-lopping, extra pegs were provided in the corridor cloakroom - some of these wooden pegs remaining in their places until the closure of the school in 1986. Enlargement of the Infant Room and improved heating proved a stumbling block for a few more years, but money was raised for a school piano by a series of evening concerts, and music became one of the strengths of the school. There were special treats; each year Sir C.J. Hubert Miller gave a Christmas treat to the whole school, if he was not abroad! As a child of nine he had left Froyle, following the death of his father, Sir Charles Hayes Miller. Following a career in the Coldstream Guards, he returned to the village, but spent a great deal of his time at his villa in Venice and, when he returned home, would visit the children with stories and gifts.

School managers and other members of the local gentry often came in and gave gifts of fruit or buns. However, the best remembered treat of the decade was probably the Queen's Diamond Jubilee. The Whitsun week's holiday was shortened by two days, so that there could be a whole week of festivities and holiday for the Jubilee in June. This included a musical festival, church services, and a special 'Schools Day' in Froyle Park on June 24th. Finally there was an extra long summer holiday of eight weeks due to an extended hop season, so by all counts 1897 was a 'summer to be remembered' by the pupils at the school. Possibly present at these celebrations was the Reverend Bridgeman H.S. Lethbridge, who was inducted as the new Vicar of St Mary's Church in October of that year. The log books tell us that he visited the school and the village earlier in the year. This photograph of him with the school is, like so many of these early images, undated, but we believe it was taken around 1898. Several of the children are wearing flowers, so perhaps it was a May Day Celebration or a Prize Giving.

The children certainly appear to be dressed in their best clothes. Frustratingly, the log books tell us nothing about this particular event. Although those little lads in the front row look as if butter wouldn't melt in their mouths, behaviour was by no means perfect. The log records instances of insolence, stone throwing, breaking slates, stealing flowers, swearing, obscene writing, etc., but the Master was reluctant to cane children unless it was really necessary. As each caning was supposed to be recorded in the log book, one can assume that it was not too common an occurrence. In cases of repeated disobedience however, he threatened to resort to his 'whip-stalk' on their buttocks, or even to 'shut them up in the shed'! Lines and detentions were often given too.

As the new century dawned, more contact was being made by head teachers of the local schools, particularly when the New Code of 1902 was to be introduced and the schools were to be taken over by County Councils.

The curriculum again broadened out, carpentry for the boys was a new subject and football was now played against other local schools. For some years individual prizes had been given by managers for subjects in which they were specially interested, but in 1903 there was the first official prizegiving, including prizes for sewing and drawing, singing, excellent conduct and perfect attendance, followed by the singing of songs and cheers for the donors of the prizes. There were now pupil's work-books for termly examinations and at the end of the year the children were placed in order of merit and seated in the class accordingly.

No mention was made of the Queen's death in January 1901 or King Edward's subsequent Coronation, but in June 1902 a week's holiday was granted by the King to celebrate the end of the Boer War. Britons were very patriotic in those times and there was great excitement when first Ladysmith, then Mafeking and finally Pretoria were relieved, with a half day's holiday granted each time. Soldiers were much in evidence in Froyle during this decade, thousands being in camp at Froyle Park for summer manoeuvres.

At this time, Captain and Mrs Sawbridge, who had been living at Froyle Park, left the village and sent down 'many useful or fancy articles to be distributed among the scholars'. Gifts to the school included a cupboard for a school museum, maps and pictures, books for a school lending library and the loan of a microscope and a magic lantern.

The school premises were to be improved; there were visits from the County Architect and an Inspector from the Surveyors Department in Winchester, followed by the enlargement of the Infant Room which was now fitted with new cupboards and a large new stove! Playground drainage was improved, to prevent flooding at the back door, (a problem throughout the school's history). Luckily the ink spill in the Master's room took place before he moved into the newly decorated Infant Room. The 'magic lantern' proved to be very useful and it was also used for evening lectures. After one 'Missionary Evening' in school, the caretaker became very irate on finding plugs of chewed tobacco on the walls and spit on the floors. His complaint was passed on to the Vicar.

The reorganisation following the Education Act of 1902 included the introduction of Form 9, a complete 'breakdown' record of children in the school in age groups, sex, etc., and details of staff and their qualifications. This form was required to be returned annually to the Department of Education, right up to the closure of the school in 1986. This information gave a much clearer idea of the schools within the County and the local authorities were able to share funding etc. more fairly. The form returned by William Downes for the year 1904 informs us that the school had been open for 421 'meetings' - presumably morning and afternoon attendances were counted separately. Luckily they had just attained the 400 mark, below which a certificate had to be included, proving that the school had been closed owing to medical reasons. Holidays during 1904 had been from March 31st - April 11th, May 20th - May 30th, August 19th - October 3rd, December 23rd - December 31st. The average attendance throughout the year had been 117 and on the last day of the year there were 140 children on the actual Admission Register. These consisted of 70 infants, 38 children between 7 years old and 12, and 31 children between the ages of 12 and 15. There was also 1 over 15, but under 16 year old. The teachers at this time were William Button Downes, a certificated teacher, with two years training in a College, and he was paid £110.00 a year. It's interesting to note that that wage had not increased in 36 years! There was one assistant teacher, namely Alice Lucy Downes, who was uncertificated and, as such, earned £55 a year. The School also had two supplementary teachers at this time - Emma Louisa Downes, who was paid £45 a year, and Bessie House, who only received £20.

This picture, taken in 1905, shows one of the school groups with those members of staff. Also in this photograph are three members of the Westbrook family. Second from left in the front row is Lilian, while next to her is William, and immediately behind him is Edith. Sadly, the next year, William died, as a result of pneumonia.

"Willie Westbrook, the seven year old son of Mr & Mrs W.H.Westbrook, died today after a considerable illness. The lad was in the infant class." *(February 1906)*

In later life Lilian wrote many articles about her childhood in Froyle and this is how she describes that awful day.

"This tragedy is as clear today in my mind, as the day it happened. Upon receiving a note from mother, the Head Master sent for my sister and together we were told to go home at once. He kindly sent an older girl with us, May Webb, she lived at Saintbury Hill Farm. How we ran that mile; over the gate into the meadow, now the Recreation Ground, over the next gate, through the orchard and home. We were taken upstairs where Mother and Father sat beside Willie's bed, we girls joined them, everything was very quiet. I touched his hand, he moved it. The next time I touched it, he did not move it, and we were told to go downstairs. So I, a child of 5 and Edith 10, had witnessed the death of our only brother.

My memory is a blank until the day of the funeral. I was in a black dress, black stockings, and boots, black ribbon in my hair and a black edged handkerchief. Likewise Sister Edith. Black horses drew the Mourning Carriages with black plumes attached to their harness. Again that same mile, as the Church was near the School. I was standing between Father's knees in the carriage and he called my attention to the school children standing outside the school with their Teachers. The picture is so clear it will never leave me. My memory ends here, no recollection of the service in the Church or at the Cemetery. Four big School boys acted as Bearers. Many folk from the village came to see him in his white coffin, some bringing their children. As I grew up I was told I nearly pulled the coffin off the bed in my eagerness to see him.

Then back at home; the drawing room full of people, relations and friends, all dressed in black, many in tears and a bewildered 5 year old in the midst of it all. I still possess the Memorial Card and envelope which Mother had given me, with my name, Lilian, written on the envelope. She made sure I also had a card like all the family far and near. Black edged with a spray of flowers and the words 'Jesus called a Little Child unto Him' on the outside of the card."

William's death was to have a profound effect on the young Lilian. Almost immediately she began to stammer. She believed it must have been because she missed him so very much. "As I grew older, the stammer was worse; the Head Master had no understanding of what I was going through. The doctor ordered that I spend the summer term, 1913, at home, which I did, feeding the chicken, collecting eggs and helping in the dairy and the washing up. Then I went to South Farnborough High School as a boarder for two years."

William Westbrook's death was certainly not an isolated case. On more than one occasion the children lined the wall of the school alongside Mr and Mrs Downes as they said goodbye to one of their friends.

"Diphtheria is developing. A child named Charles Knight died this morning and one of Munday's children has been taken to the hospital. Only 64 are present this morning, there being quite a scare in the parish. Dr Leslie, M.O.H. came over at 11.00am and formally closed the school until further notice." (October 10th 1906)

"Adelaide Steer was buried today, having died of Diphtheria." (November 9th 1908)

Following the above mentioned outbreak in the village all the desks in the school were scrubbed with carbolic soap and there was a great deal of unease amongst parents.

"Fred Cox, an infant, died this evening of Diphtheria. He was present at the treat." (February 9th 1909)

The treat referred to had taken place at Froyle Place, five days earlier. In spite of parents' low wages, 11/3½d was quickly collected for the little boy's wreath as a mark of respect from the scholars.

"School closed owing to the continued prevalence of Diphtheria." (February 26th- March 22nd 1909)

But it wasn't all sadness. There were many happy occasions, including trips to the seaside, by train from Bentley Station. As we have said, music became one of the strengths of the school; once a piano-organ was hired for the Christmas treat and a Christmas Concert was given by Lady Halle whilst staying with friends in the village. She was apparently very impressed by the children's singing and made another visit to listen to them. There were regular School Concerts, as thirteen year old Nellie Smith describes in her exercise book, in an essay she wrote in 1905.

"We had a nice concert in our school last Friday April 29th and a lot of people came to see us and to hear us sing. The band was very nice and I think the people liked it. I think the Infants did their dance drill very nice, also sung nice. The scarf drill was done by ten girls which was nice also the dumb bell drill. The three tramps was very nice too which was acted by James House, Alfred Pinnells and John Shering. The tickets were 2/- 1/- and 6d. The children's part came first and the niggers last. The two costers did theirs nice which made the people laugh. One sold herrings and oranges and the other potatoes. The people were very well satisfied with what they saw and heard. After the concert was over we all had a bun given us. All the children looked very nice and neat."

Other memorable events during the first decade of the new century included the opening of the new Froyle cemetery, the visit of the Duke of Connaught to the Aldershot Royal Review, and Empire Day ceremonies.

"Empire Day was duly observed in the schools, which were decorated with flags and union jacks. In the morning suitable instruction was given on 'The Growth of the Empire, Patriotism, Citizenship and the example of Queen Victoria'."   *(May 24th 1905)*

Nellie Smith wrote an essay on Empire Day, the following morning; she is in the photograph above, taken in 1905, but frustratingly, we don't know which of these angelic young girls she is.

"Empire Day is a new name given to the 24th May which is the late Queen's birthday. All people think of her especially on the 24th May, because she was the best and greatest Queen we ever had. Perhaps it will be put in the list of holidays next year. To remember Empire Day nearly all the schools have half a holiday and sing songs and put up their flags. The Queen reigned sixty years and if she had lived up till Tuesday Empire Day she would have been eighty six years of age. Some of the soldiers fired guns and Church bells rang to keep up the new day. We all remember how good Queen Victoria was, how she used to go and visit the poor and read the Bible to them. She said 'I will be good' and so she was until the very day of her death. But we shall never forget her and we shall think more about her on her Birthday, May 24th."

She followed this with a list of the Colonies of the British Empire, which, in 1905, were:-

"India, Ceylon, Penang, Malacca, Singapore, Labuan, North Borneo, Hong Kong, Aden, Perim, Cyprus, Cape Colony, Transvaal, Natal, Mauritius, St Helena, Ascension, Zanzibar, Australia, Tasmania, New Zealand, Pacific Islands."

Lilian Smither, nee Westbrook, who we met earlier, describes how she remembers Froyle school in the first decade of the twentieth century,

"At five years old I went to Froyle Village School with sister Edith and brother Willie, in May 1905. No mother came with us in those days. We walked through the orchard of Sylvester's Farm. Lower Froyle, then into the little meadow over the gate into the big meadow now the Village Recreation Ground, where then father's cows were grazing. I was a little scared when the cows stopped eating and looked at us. Then over, or open, the next gate into the Upper Froyle Road. We must be sure to shut the gate if we opened it, the cows would get out, then we would all be in trouble with father.

There we met up with many of the Lower Froyle children and walked the mile to School. The road in the summer was dusty and stony, in winter wet and muddy. The girls had wooden hoops and skipping ropes and the boys had iron hoops.

Arriving at school, we entered when the door was open; no lining up outside, and hung up our hats and coats. The girls always wore hats and the boys caps, and we put our dinner baskets down in the corridor. No-one took anything which did not belong to them. Our dinners were always safe.

The school had three rooms and the infants had a gallery, where we had our dinner. Some of the children were very poor in those days. We farmer's children had plenty to eat and I can see Edith giving a piece of cake or bread and butter to a child, who she knew had very little to eat. We sometimes took hard boiled eggs with bread and butter.

I won a medal at Froyle School for perfect attendance and good conduct from the Hampshire County Council, with a bar for 1912-1913, so I completed two years without missing a day.

Sometimes in the dinner hour - we had one-and-a-half hours - the older children would run to Mill Court to see the snowdrops and the river, returning in time when we heard the bell ring at 1.30 p.m.

Edith remained at the village school until she was 15; she was a monitor. I can see her now, counting each class with a slate and chalk in her hand. Her total had to agree with the Head Master. She was very tall and good looking with fair curly long hair. She was five years older than me.

The Vicar, the Reverend William Annesley, came to the school every Friday morning in term time for half an hour and instructed us on 'ancient church history'. Each child in the top classes was expected to write an essay which I did and won a book prize, Everyman's History of the English Church, dated 1909.

The Head Master was a good pianist. He taught us many patriotic songs, the National Anthem, and many other songs. Many hymns included 'Now the day is over, night is drawing nigh, shadows of the evening, steal across the sky', which we sang in the winter evenings at 4 p.m. We also started the day with a prayer and a hymn. He also taught us the Ten Commandments, 'Thou shalt not steal', and memory tells me that no-one did, and the Catechism, as in the Prayer Book, and the Creed.

Children who lived a long way away were allowed to leave school at 3.45 in Winter. The remainder left at 4 p.m., even in the darkest winter days. No mother came to collect us, we all walked to Lower Froyle without any troubles or muggings.

There was a competition in arranging wild flowers. Sister Edith won first prize several times. She had a celery glass for her arrangement. The first prize was 3s. I won the 6th prize on one occasion 6d. Many of the children used jam jars for their flowers, they also won prizes. On the same day the Fair came to the village in the field behind the play grounds. So all spectators walked through the grounds into the field beyond. What excitement, the Roundabouts, with their loud music, Swing Boats, Hoopla Stall and many other stalls of different character. Races for the Froyle school children, both boys and girls.

Now the Christmas Party at the school. The rich folk at Upper Froyle gave the children a party. We all sat in the same seats as in class. The food was good but the Christmas cake was so rich, some of us gave Rose, who sat next to me, our surplus cake and she filled her pockets to take home to give to her family a little Christmas fare. Then we were sent out into the playground, the large doors between the two classrooms were opened, then organised dances and games, this was great fun. We were all given an orange and the very poor children, food which had not been eaten. So we all walked home in the dark, every one arriving safely."

This article was written in 1990, when Mrs Smither had reached the grand age of 90. Her memory remained crystal clear, even then.

With the introduction of the 1908 Childrens Act parents had to look after their children properly or they might be taken to court. In one local case both parents were sent to prison for six weeks, evidence being given by both the local policeman and the schoolmaster of the children's neglect, with the result that the children were sent to the Alton Workhouse. The schoolmaster also appeared in court after being assaulted by a pupil's father. Three boys were repeatedly accused of stone throwing at young birds and the master punished them one afternoon. The boys refused to be caned or to speak and when the master fetched his 'whip-stalk', one boy ran out of school. The master beat the other two and reported the whole affair to the Vicar who agreed that the boys were well known in the village

Two groups of 1906. Lilian Westbrook is pictured above (front row, right)

as 'desperate', with 'bad borne influence'. Later in the evening when the Master was returning from choir practice he was violently assaulted by one of the boys' fathers. Luckily the Vicar rushing to his assistance whilst the boy concerned looked on! The Master was overcome with 'nervous prostration' and summonsed the man, going to court with the Vicar the next week. The magistrate's verdict was,

"You have committed a gross assault, by your own admission premeditated. I might have fined you £5 with the alternative of 6 months hard labour. Schoolmasters must be protected. You will pay £2 or go to prison for one month with hard labour."

The man, who appeared in court in his old working clothes, apparently whined for time to pay and was allowed a fortnight. The boy did not return to school but instead went to work with his father and apparently no efforts were made for his re-admission, to the Master's relief, one would imagine! Finally the man's employer had the family evicted from their cottage so they had to leave the village.

By now William Button Downes had become an established member of the community, sometimes being asked to undertake unusual duties such as

Mr Downes and the school football team of 1907-8

44

assisting the doctor with a child seriously injured by falling off a wagon. He was a competent organist and did relief duties at Winchester Cathedral, riding horseback home to Froyle in the early morning. He kept in touch with past pupils of the school by founding an 'Old Boy's Class' on Thursday evenings and this received a very favourable comment from Mr Milman, the local Ministry Inspector.

Life for the majority of villagers went on much as usual. Wages were low, work was hard, without any of the modern conveniences to be enjoyed by later generations. The gentry had their water heaters and flush sanitation, their motor cars and their telephones, but villagers still depended on kettles and earth closets, letter post for communication and, if lucky, a bicycle for transport or the occasional ride to town in the carrier's cart. Most winters were severe with lots of fog and snow and some late springs! Adults were becoming eager to gain more education, having attended the village school themselves as children. Gardening lectures were introduced at school in the evenings and these were popular.

The school now seemed much better provided with stock, some of which came from the National Society but the remainder from the Local Education Authority. A three monthly requisition for stock was sent to Winchester by the Master, this was usually speedily delivered, but on one occasion Mr Downes complained because ten days after the sending in of the requisition, the stocks had not arrived. Cleaning materials were requisitioned, also atlases, drawing boards and fireguards are recorded being received at one time. Educational suppliers included Arnolds and Philips & Tacey, firms still in existence at the close of the school, but needlework stock, ironmongery and fuel were ordered from local sources. Music and needlework had an important place in the curriculum and the piano was tuned regularly.

In 1909, from May to the end of July, the school was in the charge of R.Gray of the County Supply Staff, as the Master went to London to undergo ophthalmic surgery at the City Road Hospital. He returned to school in August but was to have eye problems on future occasions.

1909 also saw the death of Lady Miller, widow of the school's benefactor and mother of Sir Hubert. She was buried on 16th December in that year and the school was asked to contribute towards 'a handsome cross' as a memorial to her.

As the decade drew to a close there was correspondence regarding strengthening the staffing of the school due to changes in the Education Code. On a visit in October 1909 the Inspector had recorded,

> *"...the school is a thoroughly good one and pleasant to visit, ...but some increase in the staff will be necessary in view of the changes in the Code."*

When the managers wrote to the Education department asking for the staffing to be left as at present, the Director wrote back stating that if the staffing were not to be increased, then Article 53 of the Code must be strictly adhered to and there must be no children under five years of age in the school. This would reduce numbers and the staff position would be reviewed later. Between 1908 and 1910, numbers on books were reduced from 150 to 127, so the managers must have obeyed these instructions.

The decade ended with a relaxed happy mood throughout the school and for the first time the Master referred to the 'fun' of the last day at school before Christmas. A fortnight's holiday followed - certainly a change from the past when pupils returned to school on Boxing Day! New games were played including 'Baltona', with the whole school being instructed in the rules of the game in the playground one day and even the Infants were given a cricket set to play with. Please don't ask what the rules of 'Baltona' were, we simply do not know!

At the summer prizegiving there were the usual prizes but also medals, bars, shields and certificates from the County, the gathering was well attended by visitors and their friends, songs were sung and after the distribution of some sweets, cheers finished the afternoons proceedings. Life seemed settled with no foreboding of the changes to take place in the new decade.

A prizegiving group, date unknown
Note the 'onlookers' peeping over the fence from the Infants playground

The Great War

Sir Hubert Miller preaching to the National Reserve in 1914

In October 1910 the Vicar, Reverend Lethbridge, left the parish, and was presented with a silk umbrella by the school. His successor, Reverend William Annesley, made a good start as far as everyone was concerned by providing a gramophone concert one afternoon, which went down very well. In January the following year, Miss V.Bond joined the school staff as an uncertificated mistress in charge of Standards I and II, Mrs Downes taking standards III and IV and Mr Downes the other standards. Miss Bond's stay was a short one, as she left at Whitsun 1911 to take up a similar appointment in Lyme Regis. Her replacement Miss Gates also left after only a few months, so supply teachers took over.

Sometimes teachers from nearby schools, which had been closed temporarily because of epidemics, helped out, but the County now had its own supply staff. Miss Blakenay, Miss Kennedy and Mr Lunn were all sent but withdrawn quickly until in February 1912, Miss Trotman commenced duties.

All these changes must have worried the master and one wonders whether his own ill health effected his relationship with his staff. In March 1912 he returned to London for another ophthalmic operation, and was to remain away from his duties this time until the October of that year, Mrs Downes taking charge of the School during his absence.

Health became much more important once the School Health Services were established in 1907; there were medical inspections in school with both a school doctor and nurse in attendance, medical cards were kept up to date and clinics were held at the school or in Alton. The school weighing machine was now regularly checked and the school was visited by drill instructors and instructresses, who gave demonstration lessons of various physical exercises.

There was a whole week's holiday to celebrate the new King's Coronation in June 1911. Sir Hubert Miller attended the ceremony and spoke to the children, describing it to them; later in the week Miss Burningham brought in some Coronation souvenirs for them to look at. The following month Mr Downes must have been filled with pride when he wrote in the log book:-

"Ruth Downes has been offered a Scholarship at Eggars Girls Grammar School."   *(July 21st 1911)*

Other excitements included concerts and magic lantern shows and even fireworks in the Master's garden, attended by the older pupils, who were given gingerbread afterwards. Christmas 1912 sounds as if it was a very happy one at the School:-

"School broke up today for the Xmas holiday. Sweets and oranges distributed, the gifts of the managers. The afternoon, from 3pm, spent in festivity. Average on books 93 and infants 30. Times open 409."   *(December 1912)*

This photograph, dated 1913, may have been taken at the annual Prize Distribution in August, although, unfortunately, there is no way of knowing. However, this would account for the relatively small group and the wide range of ages within the group. In the photograph are children from two of Froyle's oldest families, the Westbrooks and the Brownjohns. We have already met Lilian Westbrook, seated far right in the second row from the front. Standing in the back row next to Mr Downes is Harold Brownjohn, while at the other end of the row are his brothers Tom and Charlie. We have actually already met their father, Alfred. He was at Froyle School between 1876 and 1882, and was featured in one of the first group photographs ever taken at the school, if you remember.

The full list of those featured above are as follows:
On the left, Mr & Mrs Downes.
Back row, left to right: Harold Brownjohn, Sidney Rix, Arthur Aslett, Hubert Brownjohn, Dick Beckhurst, Tom Brownjohn, Charlie Brownjohn.
Second row from back, left to right: Annie Munday, Edna Newport, Nellie Lawrence, Mary Munday, Alice Etherington, Lily Ellis, Daisy Page.
Second row from front, left to right: Rosie Cherrill, Kathleen Beckhurst, Tom Munday, Doris Etherington, Grace Westbrook, Lilian Westbrook.
Front row, left to right: Marjorie Cherrill, Flora Cherrill, Bill Lawrence, Ernie Munday, Bertie Gates and Ena Westbrook.

A copy of the programme for the 1913 Prize Distribution still survives, hand written in copper plate lettering:

Froyle School. Prize Distribution.
August 21st 1913
Chairman - Sir C. J. Hubert Miller, Bart.
Opening Speech.   The Chairman.
Patriotic Song.
Master's Report.
Song.   The Bells.
Distribution of Prizes.
Diocesan Awards - Prizes presented by Mrs Sedgwick.
Bishop's certificates.   Frames given by The Master.
Certificates re-signed.
Writing Prizes.   Presented by Mrs Bryan.
County Council Awards.
Sewing prizes - Presented by Mrs Summers.
Slumber Song - Girls.
Church History.   Presented by The Vicar.
Head Boy & Girl.   Prizes given by Mrs Burningham.
Voting Prizes.   Presented by Sir Hubert Miller, Bart.
Song - Killarney.
Drawing Prizes   Given by the Revd. E. Mackintosh.
Good Conduct Prizes.   Presented by Mrs Joy.
Votes of Thanks.
School Prayers.
Distribution of Sweets and Buns.

Lilian Westbrook received a medal for good attendance at one such Prize Distribution, although we are not told which one. She earned the medal by being present at school every single day for a whole year - quite an achievement!

Harold Brownjohn enjoyed his days at Froyle on the whole, apart from one lasting memory:-

"...You ask me for memories of my school days at Froyle which were happy to me on the whole. One was not so pleasant, at having to learn to write with my right hand before I was allowed to go up to the junior class at the age of six. I blame my poor writing to this as I am very much a left hander in everything else."

In 1914 the Infant classroom was finally altered and redecorated and became the classroom for the Master and older children. He was provided with a new desk and the room previously used by the staff was converted into a cloakroom.

But the shadows of war had begun to gather in 1914. Frank Binfield, an ex-scholar, joined the Royal Navy and in July of that year returned to school and spoke to the children about his life in naval barracks. School was still in session at the outbreak of the First World War but there is no record in the log book. On August 10th however, Sir Hubert Miller gave a talk to the children about 'the present war'. Apart from this, school life went on as usual, the term ended with Prize Distribution,

"a very happy afternoon, attended by eleven visitors."

A Miss Walls joined the staff in 1915, but she and Mr Downes did not get on too well and she left rather abruptly. For a short time Mr Downes' sixteen year old daughter, Ruth, helped out. The school had to be disinfected in April 1915 when a swarm of flies was recorded. Were these the same species as those which appeared in the 1980s and were dealt with by insecticide sprays as they emerged from the roof?

The First World War certainly had an impact on the village and the school, with thousands of troops being stationed in Froyle Park en route to France.

"During the week thousands of troops have been billeted in the Park and other places in the village."   *(May 14th 1915)*

William Downes felt that their presence might have had a detrimental effect on the children,

"The children seem to be more troublesome after the summer holidays than usual. Possibly the permanent presence of troops has something to do with it."   *(October 1915)*

Empire Day and Trafalgar Day became more patriotic and Sir Hubert Miller spoke regularly to the pupils on the course of the conflict. War souvenirs were collected, Mrs Sedgwick bringing in some empty shell cases from the Front, much to the delight of the youngsters.

Many families had sons who became soldiers and in 1915 an anniversary service was held to commemorate the outbreak of war a year earlier. Funds were scarce, with all available money going towards the war effort and the Master was not allowed repairs to a chimney pot or panes of glass for the school as it was in debt. Fuel supplies were also scarce and there was no Prize Distribution in 1915 or 1916.

"The prize day scheme has been abandoned.... But a good sized fruit cake and a full ¼lb of good sweets was given to each child."

In 1905 a 'Provisions of School Meals Act' had been passed, entitling needy children to a dinner at school but this was not implemented at Froyle until the beginning of the war, when meals, probably simple ones of soup and bread, were provided at the school. Later in the war Mr & Mrs Summers of Froyle Place offered to provide a hot meal for any of the school children each day at 2d a head. This was much appreciated in the village generally and most children took advantage of the scheme, with meals being served in the Summers' Racquet Court. Froyle Place was also used as a military hospital for twenty men from November 1914 until November 1915 and, after that time, was a Convalescent Home for overseas officers. One Belgian boy, whose father was a refugee being cared for there, was admitted to the school for a short time.

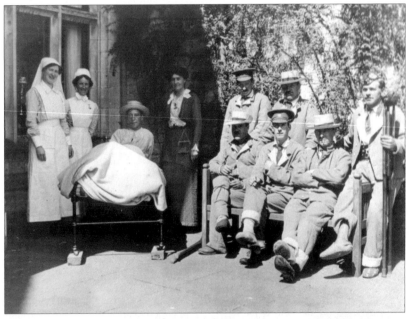

Mrs Summers, centre, with staff and convalescing servicemen at Froyle Place

For a while there seems to have been little change in the actual everyday running of the school, although everyone was caught up in the fervour of war. In 1914 and 1915 some 3 million men responded to Kitchener's famous call of "Your Country Needs You" and the thrill of watching recruits and soldiers mustering in nearby Alton was something the children never forgot.

One old age pensioner, who was seven years old at the time, remembers "My mother took us down the street to witness the events. We heard the bagpipes, saw the kilted soldiers, but were disappointed because the sentries failed to challenge us."

For them the war was no more than a game, especially when old pupils returned to the school to tell of their exploits.

"An old scholar, Cecil Sutton, now a Lieut. in the Canadian Contingent, paid a visit to the school and spoke in a most encouraging manner."   *(November 1915)*

But by the beginning of 1916, when the introduction of conscription meant that more and more fathers left the village and, one by one, families in the tightknit community were touched by tragedy, it became obvious to the older children, at least, that this was no longer a game.

The homes of Froyle suffered heavily. Mr Summers' eldest son, Captain William Asheton Summers M.C. was killed at the Battle of the Somme on the 30th July, 1916, at the age of twenty, and his name appears, with those of twenty nine other Froyle men, on the War Memorial, which stands on a hillside between the two halves of the village.

An ex Froyle school boy, Tom Aitcheson, lost his life fighting for his country. The pain felt by everyone in this small community, not just the family, is quite evident in the entry William Downes makes in his log book in November 1916,

"News has been received of the death of Lieut. Tom Aitcheson, killed in action. He was one of the best lads I ever had in any school. I had kept up a correspondence with him for years and when at home he always paid his old school a visit."

Another of those young men who never returned was Tom Brownjohn, the eighteen year old son of Mr & Mrs Alfred Brownjohn, who ran the grocers and bakers stores in Lower Froyle. The local newspaper of the time reported his death in 1918 thus,

"Private T.Brownjohn joined up in October last and was sent to the firing line after only five months training. Mr & Mrs Brownjohn received a letter from his platoon Commander:- 'In reply to your further letter of enquiry, I am sorry that I cannot give you better news. Your son was killed on top of a hill just above the Chambercy-Lary road, at 7pm on May 31st. I can't say exactly where he was buried, but it would be just in front of a line of fir trees, right at the top. Your son was very much liked by his comrades, who admired his clean healthy manner of life, and I am sure that his influence will still remain, and work for good amongst the few men left, who knew him'."

As their mothers took over the work previously done by the men, the children in school began to do their bit to 'keep the home fires burning.' In June 1915 a national War Loan Scheme had been set up to help pay for the war and many War Loan Savings Associations were formed in the schools so that the children could contribute. Every child participating was given a subscription book and when their savings reached the grand total of 15/6d they received one War Loan certificate. There was a great feeling of achievement in acquiring these certificates and school holidays were given whenever a particular goal was attained.

Nearby Bentley School had started such a scheme and, following a visit to Froyle from its Master, Mr W Skilton, a War savings Association was started at Froyle School. Another fund supported by the school children was the 'Blue Cross' (horses) fund. This particular fund, presided over by Lady Smith-Dorrien, was for the welfare of horses in wartime and would have been close to the hearts of these country children, many of whom had already seen their farm horses commandeered for use at the front.

School concerts were held on a regular basis for the wounded soldiers and sailors housed at Froyle Place and the men often reciprocated by visiting the schoolroom with exciting tales from the front line. Schoolgirls joined their mothers in the knitting craze that swept the nation. In his book 'A Social History of England', Asa Briggs tells us that 1,742,947 mufflers and 1,574,155 pairs of mittens were made for the soldiers. The number of socks is not quoted but at one stage so many had been knitted that the government felt it necessary to draw up guide lines regarding production! At Christmas food parcels containing such essentials as rice, quaker oats, potatoes, sugar and soap were sent to the troops and many pensioners still treasure the certificates they received in recognition of their small, but valuable, contribution.

Certificates like this one, presented in 1916, were treasured by their recipients

But as 1916 drew to a close there was growing concern over the shortage of food in Britain. German submarines had sunk some 632,000 tons of shipping in the last four months of the year and on February 1st 1917 their declaration of unrestricted warfare on all merchant shipping sailing to and from Allied ports forced the government to resort to vigorous economy measures. Voluntary rationing was introduced with consumers asked to limit themselves to 4lbs of bread a week, 2lbs of meat and 1lb of sugar.

The King's Proclamation on May 2nd exhorting his subjects to ".... reduce the consumption of bread in their respective families by at least one fourth of the quantity consumed in ordinary times" and "....abstain from the use of flour in pastry..." was read in school and the children asked to pledge their support. Badges were worn by those who had made a special effort to economise. With food in such short supply Britain suddenly became a nation of gardeners. During the first half of 1917 every available piece of land came under the spade and by May it was estimated that some 500,000 allotments and vegetable plots were under cultivation. "Britain has only two passions" wrote a contemporary, "to thrash the Germans and cultivate its soil."

The children soon got down to work. While the boys toiled in the allotments the girls were formed into blackberrying parties to provide jam for the soldiers. The Board of Education thought the work so worthwhile that they gave the children three half days a week simply to pick blackberries and take them to the collecting depots set up in the villages. Here they received 3d per lb for their trouble, although it is not clear whether the children or the school kept the proceeds.

An interesting side-line to all this food production was the encouragement given by the education authorities to the destruction of that gardener's enemy, the yellow cabbage butterfly! In Hampshire schools, prizes were awarded to the boys who had killed the largest number and by their efforts some 7000 butterflies were accounted for during the summer of 1918. The boys were encouraged to 'continue their good work, particularly in this time of food crisis'. May 1917 also saw the launch of a National Egg Collection and the Hampshire Herald featured this report about Froyle,

"In this village no less than 940 eggs have been sent up to the London distribution depot for the wounded and suffering sailors and soldiers. Each child, under the supervision of the staff, was allocated a district with a collecting card. Between them they collected 448 eggs and £4/2/0 in money from parishioners who did not keep fowls. This money was used to purchase fresh eggs at 2/- per dozen.

The eggs were carefully packed by the children in the boxes supplied - it is satisfactory to note that not one arrived broken at the central depot. The Parish is to be congratulated on such a happy effort to afford warmth and comfort to our brave fellows."

Later that same year it was the turn of the Admiralty to call upon the services of the country's youngsters. It was reported in the press that an urgent application had been made by the Admiralty with regard to the collection of acorns for 'a certain government manufacture' and it was hoped that the education authorities would assist by allowing the children to participate. The children of Froyle School quickly took up the challenge.

Although most people believed the acorns were destined for munitions manufacture the Imperial War Museum has no record of them being used for anything other than feeding pigs. So what this 'government manufacture' was we do not know, only that the Admiralty got all the acorns they needed and the children felt they were helping the Armed Services. With the collection of horse chestnuts, on the other hand, they really were! During the First World War some 248 million shells were used by the British Army and the Royal Navy. The basic propellant used to fire these shells, and for a whole host of other military purposes, was cordite. The solvents used in manufacturing cordite were acetone and ether-alcohol. Acetone was produced almost entirely by the destructive distillation of wood and the world market in this commodity was dominated by the great timber growing countries. Before the war acetone was mainly imported from the United States, British manufacturers simply could not compete successfully with foreign makers and our own plants were both small and antiquated.

In 1913 a modern factory was established in the Forest of Dean but by the outbreak of the war in August 1914 the stocks of acetone for military use stood at only 3,200 tons and it was soon apparent that this and existing production would not meet the rapidly growing demands which was mainly caused by the increased requirement for cordite. It was found that acetone could be produced from potatoes and maize and new plants were erected to undertake this work.

By 1917, however, the German submarine offensive in the Atlantic caused a shortage of freight which threatened to cut off supplies of North American maize. Faced with the possibility of a serious maize shortage, experiments were begun to find a substitute for it in acetone production and it was discovered that the horse chestnut could be used as an alternative. Factory experiments were set in hand and the site chosen for the project was the Synthetic Products Company, King's Lynn, which had been converted for the production of butyl-alcohol and acetone from potatoes in 1915. Successful results indicated that the manufacture of acetone from horse chestnuts could be achieved and the Ministry of Munitions commenced the task of organizing the collection and transport of 1917 horse chestnut 'harvest'.

A statement in The Times of 26th July 1917 read, "...chestnut seeds, not the green husks, are required by the Government for the Ministry of Munitions. The nuts will replace cereals which have been necessary for the production of an article of great importance in the prosecution of the War."

The major method of collection was to enlist the aid of school children. Vast quantities of horse chestnuts were collected but only 3,000 tins reached the King's Lynn plant. Collection was restricted by transport difficulties and letters in The Times tell of piles of rotting horse chestnuts at railway stations. The columns of The Times also reflect another aspect of this story. Nobody really knew why they were collecting horse chestnuts. The government was, naturally, reticent to reveal the motive behind its scheme since the Germans could very well copy this novel form of acetone production.

Froyle School and its adjoining Schoolhouse in the early 1900s

Back at Froyle School attendances and absences were now mentioned less often in the log book but, at one stage, the Director of Education requested the Vicar to refer to 'The Green Book of Instructions' over absences of pupils to sing in the church choir and he also refused to allow the Master's daughter, Ruth, a mark in the register the day she visited Eggar's School for an interview. In 1917 the Master reported the girls for 'becoming much rougher', followed by the comments that a Girl Guide Company had recently been formed in the village. Did this imply cause and effect, one wonders? The days of equality had not yet arrived but on March 9th, 1917, the girls and boys thoroughly enjoyed the snow fight they were allowed having both made forts in the playground following a heavy fall of snow.

There was a serious influenza epidemic at the end of 1918 which interrupted the return of the school to peace-time conditions. Children now had to continue in school full time until fourteen years old and half time schooling was no longer allowed. Attendance charts for groups of local schools were published, Bentley coming 1st with 95% attendance, Froyle being 7th with 93%. School photographs were resumed and a 'Travelling Dairy Show' visited the village, allowing three girls at a time to attend lessons on 'cheesemaking' and other dairy topics. A cookery class was organised by the County at the Racquet Court, Froyle Place, but this was transferred to Hamble on the resignation of the Instructress. Fuel was in very short supply and the school was closed at times if the thermometer fell too low.

Lectures given in school at this time included 'The Dardanelles', 'Bolshevism', and 'The Navy League', but gradually life in the village was restored to normality. Sir Hubert Miller resumed his visits abroad and spoke on topics such as 'Italy' and 'Venice' once more. One excitement at this time was the descent of a balloon in Froyle Park - many children truanted to see it but were punished the next day by Mrs Summers refusing to serve them a school meal! The Master was heartened by this backing up of his authority.

During the last year of the war, London children were admitted to the school as they moved away from the 'air-raid zones'. These children were able to return home later in 1918 and finally the war ended on November 11th, 1918. A thanksgiving service was held in St Mary's Church and peace celebrations were later held on July 19th, 1919, including sports events.

So drew to a close the war to end all wars. As they sang and danced at the peace celebrations in July 1919 little were those Froyle children to know that in just 20 years they would once more receive the call to serve their King and country; but this time the sacrifice and the glory would be theirs.

All Change

The girls show off their new maypole in 1923

A nd so a new decade began and life in school returned to some kind of normality. Luxuries such as cars and telephones began to appear. Mrs Summers used her telephone to obtain fuel supplies for the school on one occasion and one of the school children's parents was a 'motor driver' for Mr Summers.

In the village itself, plans were soon under way for some permanent memorial to all those who had given their lives in the Great War. Sir Hubert Miller was the chairman of the Memorial Committee and the treasurer, Rev Annesley, collected donations throughout the village during 1920. On April 14th, 1921, the cross, erected on high ground overlooking the village, was dedicated by the Bishop of Guildford. The Hampshire Herald reported, "Among the wreaths laid on the plinth was a handsome cross of arum lilies encircled by laurel leaves, subscribed for by the teachers and scholars of Froyle School, 'In grateful remembrance of all they did for us.' Fourteen of the names on the stone were those of former scholars."

Nelson Aitcheson
Thomas Aitcheson
William Ayres
Andrew Binfield
Frederick Binfield
Tom Brownjohn
Reginald Cooper
Charles Hillier
Robert Hillier
David Hounsham
Frank Hounsham
Charles Ivil
Frederick Knight
Wilfrid Messenger
Edward Mitchell

James Neale
Frederick North
James Oakley
Frederick Oliver
Henry Pinnells
William Pinnells
Robert Scrivener
Herbert Sherville
Gladstone Steer
Albert Stratton
William Summers
Richard Vickery
Albert Ward
Albert Webb
Percy Yalden

Throughout the rest of the 1920s the children always attended the War Memorial on Armistice Day.

> *"Armistice Day. The children observed the two minutes silence. They also placed a laurel wreath on the War Memorial and sang Kipling's Recessional. Colonel Edwards addressed the children on 'Our duty as Englishmen'."*   *(T.Knight, November 11th 1925)*

By now teachers pay and conditions were improved. However, Mr Downes was not a well man and his wife was not in the best of health either. By the Autumn of 1921, with Mr Downes in London for more treatment on his eyes and Mrs Downes unwell, the school was run for some weeks by Mr Arthur

Eelson. Mr Eelson was the Headmaster of West Meon School and his own school was closed during this time due to an epidemic. He drove by car from West Meon each day, frequently opening the school late because of 'engine-trouble'. Mr & Mrs Downes returned at the beginning of December for two weeks but Mrs Downes then found herself in charge as the.....

"Master was suffering from an acute nervous breakdown."

The Spring term of 1922 saw a series of teachers in charge of the school, beginning with Mr William Sydney Chisman, who began teaching at Froyle on January 23rd. Two days later he had an accident while riding his bicycle, so his Acting Headship must have been one of the shortest on record! Mrs Downes found herself in charge of the school yet again and finding the responsibility too much for her,

"Our Doctor says the strain is too great for me." *(January 1922)*

Miss Alice Stillman took charge of the school on February 3rd, followed by Mr Thomas Stroud on 13th February. Mr Stroud remained at Froyle for just over a month and appears to have been very interested in weather reporting! Nearly every one of his entries in the log book mentions the weather - on 20th February he couldn't even get to the school,

"owing to heavy and continuous rain."

The following week there was a school closure to mark the occasion of Princess Mary's marriage. The day after the children were shown the,

".....illustrated papers dealing with the wedding and a lesson of information given."

Mr Stroud's own school in Rowledge had been closed owing to an epidemic, and he returned to it towards the end of March.

Inevitably that Spring Term of 1922 was both an unsettled and an unhappy term, culminating in William Button Downes' final entry in the log book on March 21st 1922,

"Resigned the mastership of these schools following upon a serious nervous breakdown." and signed, *"William Downes."*

Mr J.R.Sutherland took over as staff supply on 22nd March and was concerned that some parents were encouraging rudeness in their children. He faced an uphill struggle trying to restore discipline amongst children who had been taught by so many different teachers during the previous six months.

Mr Downes' wife and sister remained teaching at the school for another month, retiring on April 21st 1922. Thus ended a thirty year span of a school ably run, until those last few months, by a conscientious and caring Master, helped by his family throughout the years. The school photographer called on June 30th .

And then on July 31st 1922 arrived the man who became known not just as a good Headmaster, but also as Froyle's Historian, Mr Tom Knight.

Miss Pullinger had already joined the staff in May as an Infant teacher and Mrs Jesse Bygrave started work on 14th August that same year. Between them, these three provided stability and continuity in the school for the next thirty four years.

Mr Knight was very busy at the start of his mastership - he discovered the H.M.I. report in the Master's desk soon after his arrival and realised the uphill task ahead of him. It stated that,

"The school has suffered somewhat owing to the fact that during the last two years of his thirty years of good service Mr Downes was not a well man and for the past five months has not been in school at all. Supply teachers had done their best to cope and work is, on the whole, creditable."

School records were all waiting to be made up, supplies needed, both books and stationery and needlework and cleaning materials, also fuel in short supply! A school concert and closure was arranged for the last day of the Autumn Term for school funds. Permission for the closure was at first refused by the Director of Education but he later relented.

Mr Knight was highly respected by all those he taught. Don Pritchard, who was at Froyle School from 1922 until 1931, remembered him well, "Mr Knight was a good Headmaster, but very strict. He wouldn't allow any talking at all. We used to sit in pairs in iron framed desks. His favourite expression was 'Come out, you scamp!' He would tell us wonderful stories about his time in East Africa. When he mentioned that, we knew we were all right for the afternoon. He once said, in later years, 'You were a rough lot, but I wouldn't have swapped you for the world!'"

This photograph of Mr Knight and his wife was taken in the garden of the Schoolhouse.

Mr and Mrs Knight had a daughter, Barbara, who attended Froyle School. At first the children used to run after her, calling "You're a ghost! You're a ghost!" This was because the ghost of one Barbara Knight, who lived and farmed at Sylvesters in Lower Froyle in the late 1800s, was said to be seen walking on the lawn of the house on Midsummer Eve. Why she walked no-one knew. She may still do so to this day!

In 1923 the Duke and Duchess of York were married and Froyle School was given a holiday to celebrate the occasion. Two of the managers of the school, Mrs Summers and Mrs Sedgwick, presented it with a maypole, so that maypole dancing could be part of the celebrations.

Naturally, a special photograph was taken of them using the maypole for the first time. A young Mrs Bygrave can be seen on the extreme right.

The playground was cleaned up, the 'offices', as the toilets were always called, were inspected more regularly, with frequent need for more 'dry earth' or new pails! Mr Knight set great store by clean 'offices' and was always mentioning them in the log book. One of the first things he did on taking over as Headmaster was to examine the 'offices' and arrange for all the seats to be scrubbed. The school doctor and nurse now visited regularly for inspections and eye clinics were held at Mrs Summers' Racquet Court. The Racquet Court was where Mrs Summers always provided a Christmas treat for the children of Froyle School. This took the form of tea and an entertainment and was a tradition which was to continue with future residents of Froyle Place. These special treats at 'the Big House' were never forgotten by the youngsters.

In March 1923 Mr Knight was concerned about the children's welfare and requested gifts of old boots and shoes, to replace some of their worn out footwear. You only have to look at these two photographs, the first taken in 1922 and the second in 1924, to see the difference his plea for new boots has made. It is obviously a little difficult to see without a magnifying glass, but the boots of the children in the 1922 photograph are looking a little scuffed to say the least.

In the 1924 photograph, below, the boots are so shiny and new you could almost see your face in them!

In May 1923 the village policeman visited the school following complaints that a lot of damage was being done to the allotments. The blame was put firmly on the local gypsies until one youngster owned up that he had been helping himself to a few cauliflowers when nobody was looking. What he actually did with them was never explained.

In this 1923 photograph we can see Florence Lee, who attended Froyle School from 1921-30. She is standing, wearing a white pinafore, immediately behind the fourth boy from the left, sitting with his legs crossed. On this particular day, Flo, as she was always known, is still wearing her pinafore, which is quite unusual, as she explains,

"I used to have to wear a white pinny. How I hated wearing it. As soon as I got to school I took it off and hid it in my dinner bag. I used to take egg sandwiches for my lunch. I carried them in a little tin case. I can remember it well - it was grey with white lines. I remember my friend, Dolly Emblyn, always had corned beef, so we would swap sandwiches. We always walked to school together. When we got to school we hung our lunch boxes on our pegs and our coats on top of them."

Don Pritchard also remembered lunch times in the 1920s, "There were no school dinners. We used to bring sandwiches to school. I remember one boy liked bread and jam and egg! We used to take oxo and make ourselves a hot drink." Don also remembered these songs from the 20s.

"Cold the blast may blow, heaping high the snow,
Winds may loudly roar, may loudly roar........."

And another of his favourites,

> "There's a merry brown bird singing up in the tree,
> He's singing to me, he's singing to me.
> And what does he say, little girl, little boy?
> All the world's running over with joy."

On July 2nd 1923 May Cooper, standing third from right in this group of 1920, began working as a monitress, assisting Mrs Bygrave. She received a salary of £15 a year.

"Mr Knight offered to take me as a Pupil Teacher when I was 14. He lent me his books and I took a correspondence course - one way teachers were trained in those days - I had 25 shillings a month book allowance. I used to teach with Mrs Bygrave. She was very keen on Amateur Dramatics, so we put on some pretty good shows. Ena Westbrook formed a Netball team, so we walked all over the place to play matches on Saturdays." (May Cooper, 1915-25)

There was a great deal of singing at the 1924 Prize Giving on June 6th, when Mrs Summers and Mrs Sedgwick provided buns, sweets and oranges for the children. Altogether 41 children received prizes or certificates for work or attendance and the grand sum of £8/14/6 was spent on their prizes, with the money having been raised at a number of school concerts. After the presentation the children sang songs - probably the very ones Don remembered - and twenty four girls gave a display of maypole dancing in the playground. As Mrs Summers was not able to attend the actual event she promised a proper treat later on. On the 24th June she kept her word and paid the expenses for twenty two children and four teachers to go to the British Empire Exhibition at Wembley. One can imagine the excitement felt, not just by the children, but by the staff themselves, as the party set out from Bentley Station. Presumably, Mr Knight did not go with them, as there is no mention in the log book of the actual trip, although, no doubt, several essays would have been written on the subject over the next few weeks. What the children would have seen on that special day out is described in "A Twentieth Century Scrapbook",

"It cost ten million pounds to construct a miniature British Empire at Wembley. The 1924 Exhibition was designed as a gigantic showcase for imperial wealth and prosperity but, in retrospect, it was also the last grand fling of an Empire in decline. The buildings, including the sports stadium which later earned a reputation as the home of greyhound racing, covered 220 acres. Among the more impressive pavilions was the Palace of Engineering which was six and a half times the size of Trafalgar Square and the largest concrete construction in the world. The Indian exhibits were housed in a replica of the Taj Mahal, Ceylon displayed a collection of pearl necklaces insured for a million pounds and Canada produced a life-size statue of the Prince of Wales, made of butter. One of the most popular novelties was the Queen's Dolls House, a complete mansion built to the scale of one inch to the foot. Leading artists and crafts men had taken two years to complete it. So detailed was the design that the library, 22 inches high, contained 170 books bound in red and grey leather. Many of them were written in manuscript by their authors who included Rudyard Kipling, Arnold Bennett, Thomas Hardy and Joseph Conrad. The Wembley Exhibition was opened on 23rd April 1924 and about one hundred thousand sightseers turned up on the first day. On Whit Monday, despite an unofficial underground strike, three times that number of visitors packed the avenues and pavilions. The demand for tickets was such that it was decided to open the Exhibition for a second year and when it finally closed, in October 1925, wonderful Wembley 'went to the dogs'. The Empire, it was said, followed suit."

The Inspector's report for 1924 commented on the hard working conscientious staff and stated that standards were improving. The low classification in the school meant high numbers in the lower standards and the Master was asked to accelerate the movement of children to higher classes, but it was pointed out in the report that the low classification was partly due to the migratory character of the school population.

In spite of staff illness, bad weather and further epidemics, by 1927 almost every one of the 103 children in the school had been promoted and the Master was congratulated on the progress of the scholars. The school was cleaner, after a succession of caretakers; it was certainly warmer too, with more regular fuel stocks arriving, and the classroom stoves having been overhauled.

The Master suffered a six week illness in the early summer and the school was in the charge of Mr A.R.B.Cook. On Mr Knight's return the school was inspected by an H.M.I. (Mr E.Wynn-Williams) and the report stated, *"the Headmaster and his staff are to be congratulated on the state of the school."*

1928 saw pupil numbers beginning to rise and when, by the beginning of March, they had risen to 121, Mr Knight felt it was time to make the managers aware of the overcrowding. Aware they may have been, but nothing appears to have been done about the situation. Work was carried out, however, to improve the school building itself. On August 8th a Village Fete was held to raise funds for new floors for the school. This event was obviously a resounding success, as the new floors were laid in two classrooms during the summer holidays. The 'offices' were improved at the same time. In March 1929 a new fence was erected between the playgrounds. Whether this new fence resulted in the boys being forbidden to kick their footballs about or not, we don't know, but in July of that year ten year old James (Jim) Knight, no relative of Mr Knight, wrote in his exercise book,

"Letter to Col.Innes   29/7/29
Dear Sir,
    For the past six months you have allowed the boys of this school to play cricket and football in your park which is opposite Froyle School. This has been appreciated by all concerned. We promise that we will not throw paper about and make the field look untidy. Our playground is not big enough for us to play cricket and football in.
    Yours respectfully,
        James Knight"

Whether this was simply an exercise, or whether the letter was sent, we do not know. Colonel Innes rented Froyle Place until 1933, so possibly the boys had the use of part of the park until at least then. There is no record in the log book. This photograph of Jim Knight, with his sister Nancy, was an official school photo taken in about 1929.

The decade ended with epidemics of measles, chicken pox and mumps. On 9th December only 23 of the 102 children on the roll were present in school.

The Winning Years

The Folk Dancing team perform at Rotherfield Park on 20th July 1935

The Decade began with a good H.M.I. report, which must have pleased Tom Knight. *"This is a good school."*

It was a time of change and excitement in the village. Jim Knight wrote in his exercise book,

"Modernising Froyle 3/3/30

Electric light cables are being laid up the Hen and Chicken Hill in Upper Froyle, because some people want it. It is very convenient to have it, but it will be too dear for some people, as it costs ninepence per unit. At Lower Froyle gas pipes are being laid from Isington crossroads and I think they are coming to Upper Froyle. The men have got as far as Mr Brownjohn's shop. After the men have finished laying the pipes and cables the roads are going to be widened and in later years I expect that the roads will be tarred. People will be able to have better lighting in their houses and some will be having gas stoves for cooking."

He also described his classroom in 1930,

"The Senior Room of Froyle School is at the south-west end of the school, and it used to be the Infant Room. It was lengthened, and made nearly twice as long, and since then it has been the Senior Room. There are three blackboards and easels in the room and also a stove near the door. Also there is a piano made by the British Piano Company Ltd, London, standing at the bottom end of the room. At the south-west end of the room there is a big oriel window, but there are also eight oblong windows. There are three square cupboards, two of which are near the door, and over the door is a crescent shaped flag. On the wall is a Swiss clock."

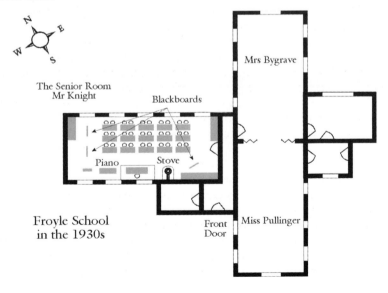

In June 1930 a Froyle pupil was offered a special place in Secondary Education as a result of the exam taken in March. Her parents decided that they could not accept the offer. No doubt the thought of the extra cost of school uniforms, books, games kit etc, plus the knowledge that their daughter would be expected to remain at school from 14-16 influenced their decision. Some parents would not even allow their children to sit the examination and many adults actually felt that the use of higher education to ordinary children was doubtful and likely to cause barriers between parents and their children. These decisions probably benefited most rural schools who, like Froyle, still kept most of their pupils till the age of 14. Secondary schools increased throughout the Country in the 'thirties' and the Education Act of 1936 declared that by September 1939 all post 11year old children should move to one of three types of secondary school - grammar, modern or technical - and stay there until 15 or 16, but the Act failed to be implemented because of the outbreak of the war.

Teachers' salaries and conditions of employment improved during the pre-war decade; meagre salaries, plus poor promotion prospects and a poor public image had led to a shortage of trained teachers. In 1914 their salaries had been £127 per annum for men and £95 for women, but within twenty years the salaries rose to £310 for men and £254 for women. There was also provision for a pension at 60+ for those with at least 30 years of service, as well as a 'Burnham Scale' for negotiation of teachers salaries by a special committee. Teacher status was now comparable with civil service, local government and other 'white collar' workers.

Children's health in the thirties was improving, although diphtheria and scarlet fever could still be fatal infections and measles, whooping cough and mumps were serious although quite commonplace. There were still 'Isolation Hospitals' for infectious diseases, most areas were within easy reach of 'Cottage Hospitals' now with children's wards. Research had taken place to find vaccines for the above infections and diphtheria immunisation is mentioned in the log book for 1937. Poliomyelitis was another dreaded infection, but of course children still also suffered from lesser infections such as ringworm and impetigo. Vermin were still plentiful and children were regularly excluded by the school nurse for head lice and sometimes body fleas. Regular visits by the Schools' Medical Officer and the school nurse meant a better check on the children's health, but many still came from poor families, existing on a very basic diet, often supplemented by their own animal or vegetable produce. Dairy foods were comparatively expensive and children who lacked these foods were likely to suffer from rickets through calcium deficiency in their bones. There were many chest troubles including consumption, which could be contracted from untreated cows milk - hence the introduction of Tuberculin Tested herds and milk. Bronchitis and pneumonia were fairly common, often as a result of poor living conditions. Extreme poverty had gone in most cases and unemployed people could claim 'dole-money' but for many families it was still a struggle to live, eat, be clothed and keep a roof over their heads, particularly if they had lots of children, in the days before 'Family Allowance'. Things were sometimes easier in rural areas, where there were tied farm cottages and sometimes free milk, but agricultural wages were still low and the work was heavy and mostly manual, and children's help was required on the farms at various times. Travellers and hop-pickers came to the village at times, but these children did not always attend school regularly and therefore missed health checks. The School Dentist now also visited schools often - too often, the children would tell you! His visit was very necessary in July 1931, when out of 98 pupils examined, no less than 80 needed dental attention! As dental treatment had previously only been given at the dental clinic in Alton, all the onus was on parents to get their children to and from the town - there were probably many cases of toothache at this time. By 1938 however, mention is made of a 'dental van near the school' and mobile dental treatment continued until the close of the school in 1986.

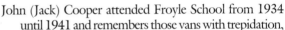

John (Jack) Cooper attended Froyle School from 1934 until 1941 and remembers those vans with trepidation, "We hated the visit of the dentist who came in a caravan which was parked up at Froyle Place. If you had to visit him you were thankful if your name came early in the alphabet. The drill was worked by a foot pedal. Later in the day his feet got tired and the drill went slower!"

In later years the technology may have improved but the arrival of the dentist's caravan was still one of the more unhappy memories of schooldays spent at Froyle.

Annual reports on the work of the school by H.M.I.s continued to be good, particularly that of 1933. The curriculum in the pre-war years however was still very regimented, although new ideas were percolating through. Although Mr Knight was a progressive man, and in October 1934 changed to a 'New Timetable', on trial, there was a return to the old timetable by the summer of the next year, as the new timetable was not proving satisfactory. It would be interesting to know the contents of both timetables, but, alas, there is no record!

The usual primary school day in the thirties commenced with Assembly and R.E., followed by P.E., in rows in the playground, and Sums for an hour before playtime. This would be followed by English mostly, with other subjects, History, Geography, Nature Study, Drawing, Needlework, Handwork and Games occupying the afternoons; this timetable was religiously adhered to in most schools.

Margaret Wye, nee Young (1924 -1931) remembers the 'exercises' the children did in the playground. Occasionally they gave displays at the local Fete, as in the photograph above, taken, we believe, in 1931 - she is second from the right. Myrtle Lee (1925-1932) also remembers those displays,
"The music was supplied by an old fashioned gramophone. I remember we always ended up the display by forming the letters FS for Froyle School. In the picture you should see E.Butler, J.Rix, D.Childs, M.Herson, M.Cox, N.Knight, D.Pinnells, D.Herson, D.Holland, A.Childs, A.Shaw, P.Newland, L.Young, M.Young, P.Savage, J.McDonnell, P.Fry, D.Brogden, M.Caines, G.Cherryll, M.Lee, L.Knight, D.Pritchard, R.Robinson, D.Pocock, W.Harris, W.Hill, W.Rhodes, G.McDonnell, A.Rhodes, R.Morse, D.Rix, J.Stenning, L.McKemblin."

In January 1932 twelve boys benefited from 'Agricultural Instruction'. This consisted of one week of 'Theoretical Instruction' in school, followed a week later by 'Practical Instruction' on a neighbouring farm.

"Miss Griffiths commenced a course of Agricultural Instruction with 12 senior boys:-

Leonard Knight	*Stanley Valentine*
Douglas Rix	*Frank Rhodes*
George McDonnell	*Raymond Morse*
Alec Wells	*William Harris*
Reginald Morgan	*Ronald Aldridge*
William Pritchard	*Herbert Blanchard"*

73

Two classes of 1930

Mr Knight himself (seen below) took the boys for School Gardening, which commenced in November 1932 and occupied two hours a week in place of Nature Study and Handwork. The School Gardens Officer, Mr J.O'Carroll, visited the school frequently to encourage and advise and his reports were very favourable, particularly the April 1934 report which said,

"A small garden but interesting because of the keenness of the teacher and the excellence of the instruction. In addition to flowers, vegetables are well grown. A First Class Garden!"

He also commented on the glass cloches acquired to enable winter lettuce to be grown. Even fruit trees were planted.

It's interesting to take a look at a page from the school's requisition book for 1932. Besides all the usual items such as scissors, plasticine, pins, penholders, brushes, etc. we find a page dedicated to garden tools. Mr Knight, ordered and received 10 spades, 10 forks, 5 hoes, 10 Dutch hoes, 10 rakes, 5 trowels, 5 small forks, 5 dibbers, 2 pairs of shears, 1 watering can, 1 reel and line, 1 wheelbarrow, 5 hand hoes and 2 large14 inch iron rakes. A note in the margin of this page tells us that the entire stock of garden tools was sent to Alton Senior School on 18th April 1946. This coincided with the retirement of Mr Knight and was possibly because the gardening classes had made use of the garden belonging to the schoolhouse. From 1947 this building accommodated staff of the Lord Mayor Treloar College, which had recently purchased Froyle Place and the Miller Estate.

In January 1933 the girls had their turn - Miss Broadbent, Domestic Science Officer, commenced a course for girls at the Institute Hut in Lower Froyle, to teach them basic cookery and housewifery. Mornings were spent at the Institute but the girls were in school for the afternoons.

"We had a month long course of Domestic Science. There were fifteen girls and I always remember Miss Broadbent teaching us to 'scrub to the grain of the wood'." (Mary Caines, 1927-36)

But it was needlework and country dancing that really made the1930s the 'winning years' for the school, thanks to the enthusiasm and expertise of Mrs Jesse Bygrave. Margaret Young told us, "Mrs Bygrave was a perfect teacher and

75

it was her instruction in the art of tapestry I will always be grateful for. All my family now has a picture of my making."

In 1933 the school entered a national competition for needlework and found themselves amongst the prizewinners. The Froyle Parish Paper of St's Mary & Joseph announced the results with pride,

"We take off our hats to Mary Caines, aged 11 years, who won second prize in the junior class for plain needlework in the National Needlecraft Competition recently held by the 'School Mistress'. The Competition was open to schools in the British Isles and abroad, and attracted thousands of entries. In the same class, certificates of honourable mention were gained by Marjorie Herson and Nancy Knight, while in the senior section a similar certificate was won by Dorothy Herson. Ordinary certificates for plain needlework were awarded to Marjorie Cox and Jessie Pinnells and a certificate for embroidery to Peggy Newland.

This is certainly a great accomplishment and worthy of loud cheers, so let us give three hearty cheers for the successful children, coupled with one extra loud one for Mrs Bygrave who has been untiring in her efforts of training and supervision."

Three of the girls who were so successful share their memories of that competition with us,

Mary Caines, seated,
with her brother and sister

"I don't remember what I made, only that the stitches were so tiny you could hardly see them. As well as the certificate, I won £1 and a lovely cream lace collar." (Mary Caines, 2nd prize in the Junior section)

"We were told by Mrs Bygrave that Queen Mary had visited the Exhibition and seen our work. Most of my work, which was a petticoat, was done by gas-light at home, by a coal fire. I don't know how I kept it clean." (Dorothy Herson, Certificate of Honourable Mention)

"My entry was a full length short sleeved nightdress in plain white Nainsook, edged with mauve bias binding. I remember getting into trouble with Mrs Bygrave because I pricked my finger and she was worried I would mark my needlework." (Marjorie Cox, Certificate for plain needlework)

A special prize day was held on June 14th 1933, when the awards were presented to the girls by the Hon.Mrs Parsons. According to the log book, some sixty parents and friends visited the school to see the needlework and the school gardens.

In 1935, once more under the instruction of Mrs Bygrave, the school entered the National Needlework Competition again and this time went one better, with young Jean McDonnell taking first prize in the Junior section with her 'lingerie garment entirely hand made'. In the same class Nancy Knight and Dora Holland each received Certificates of Honourable Mention and Peggy Robinson a Certificate of Merit. Nancy Knight also received a Certificate of Honourable Mention for her hand made outer garment and a Certificate of Merit for a canvas embroidery in wool. In the senior classes Marjorie Herson received two Certificates of Honourable Mention for lingerie and an outer garment. She also received a Certificate of Merit for a canvas embroidery in silk.

Mrs Bygrave had more success that year when a team of fifteen of her girls found themselves taking first place honours in the English Folk Dancing Competition, held that year in Guildford. The photograph below sees them at the East Tisted Fete in Rotherfield Park on 20th July 1935, when they gave a display of their expertise. Just look at those hemlines! Have you ever seen anything so level? The reason for this was that all the dresses had to have the hemlines adjusted so that they were all the same height off the ground. Notice how they even co-ordinate with the length of the outfit being worn by Mrs Bygrave.

The girls are (left to right) Sheila Hill, Dora Holland, Rose Willis, Doris England, Violet Harris, Olive Rix, Nancy Knight, Peggy Robinson, Mary Burns, Marjorie Herson, Marjorie Watterson, Violet Wells, Jean McDonnell and Phyllis Savage.

Country dancing in general was very popular. Joan Andrew (1933-1939) was just one youngster who loved maypole dancing in particular, as did Dorothy Rix, nee Herson (1925-1934),

"One of my happiest memories of school is dancing round the maypole. We were all dressed to match the ribbons of the actual maypole - red, white, blue, green and yellow. The outfits were all made by Mrs Bygrave. She was a wonderful needlewoman."

Dorothy (Dolly) Attwood, nee Cooper (1931-1940) remembers, "I loved Country Dancing but couldn't go away to competitions because my parents wouldn't let me go. I also loved needlework and I made my own country dancing dress. Once Mrs Bygrave brought in some sewing for some pupils who didn't have any and they spent time mending her husband's longjohns! We also did knitting, using four needles to knit gloves."

In the classroom there was more movement and freedom for the Infants, who were taught by Miss Pullinger. It was even suggested that the children might sometimes sit on mats instead of chairs and those very same straw mats survived up to the end of the school's life! One criticism of the Junior class by the Inspectors was their lack of reading, apart from comics! but many homes had few children's books at that time, although children could borrow books from their local libraries. Books had fewer illustrations and no attractive paper covers in pre war days so would not attract reluctant readers. They were however often given as school and Sunday school prizes, so many children had a small collection.

The school possessed very little equipment - there was a wind-up gramophone for the Country Dancing, but no audio-visual equipment otherwise. Even a radio had to be borrowed - as on the occasion of the proclamation of King Edward VIII as the successor to George V, who died in January 1936, when the Vicar loaned a portable wireless for the broadcast. The Vicar addressed the pupils on the death of the King and a day's holiday was granted on the funeral day. There had been a holiday to celebrate King George V's Silver Jubilee in 1935 by extending the Whitsun break, a day to celebrate the wedding of the Duke of Kent, and later, after a troubled period over the Royal Family, a celebration day's holiday for the Coronation of King George VI. Later in 1937 the school was closed for a day when the premises were used as a polling station.

Numbers of pupils during the decade dwindled from 120 to 80. There was less absenteeism as winters seemed to be wet rather than too cold. Holidays were now organised by the County and consisted of about two weeks at Christmas, two at Easter, one week at Whitsun and five weeks in the Summer, sometimes divided between corn and hop harvests. The children during the decade were very patriotic; Armistice Day was always remembered on the actual day by the customary two minutes silence at 11a.m.

The staff during this time remained constant, although Mr Knight and Mrs Bygrave both had spells of illness when supply teachers were obtained via the County Education Office.

In August 1934 a student from the Battersea Polytechnic College spent a month on teaching practice at the school. Caretaking standards varied considerably with many different caretakers and the Headmaster spent much time in checking their work and inspecting the 'offices'.

There were still not many cars in rural areas before the war but more people obtained bicycles and cycling permits were granted by the Headmaster just before the war, enabling older children to ride their bicycles to school. Jack Cooper remembers, " The cycling permits were, I think, a County requirement. One had to apply for permission to bring a bicycle on to school property. A test - in my case conducted by Mr Knight - consisted of checking ones ability to 'ride, steer and brake', together with the ability to touch the ground whilst still sitting on the saddle. The brakes were checked as were the tyres and the cycle was checked for loose nuts, bolts, etc. A successful pass gave one a written certificate of competence and a permit to have a cycle on school property. Riding a cycle on school property was absolutely forbidden - one had to mount and dismount on the road outside and push the cycle to the cycle sheds in the boys playground behind Mrs Bygrave's classroom."

Jack's memories of those days are so vivid that we share more of them with you here.

"My stay at Froyle was not as long as some. I arrived in the district at the age of seven when my family took up employment with Ernest James Longman, a farmer from Binsted, who farmed four farms in the area. As my family was employed at Mill Court Farm we lived at Mill Court in the Mill Cottage by the river and were actually in Binsted parish but, at the age of 7, I started school at Froyle because it was that much nearer. At this time, 1934, there were at least 6 children attending Froyle School from Mill Court - Basil Lee, Victor Stratton, Harold Rowell, John Willis, Snowdrop Willis (who never used her first name always being called 'Snowball') and myself. It was then that I first met the rather formidable Mrs Bygrave, always referred to as 'Teacher' or 'Ma'am' except in the playground when she was always 'Jesse'. Also Mr Knight, the Headmaster, known out of school as 'Tommy'. He was one of the fairest and most dedicated men that I think I have ever met, always providing that one could tolerate his many 'When I was in East Africa....' stories. The School Museum, which was located on the top of a large wooden bookcase just inside the senior classroom, contained much of the items that he brought back with him.

As I was aged 7 I did not have contact with Miss Pullinger, the Infants Teacher, who, as far as I remember, did not have a school 'nickname'. She cycled each day from Alton. Mrs Bygrave came from Aldershot by train to Bentley station and then by cycle to Froyle. I can never remember either being late!

My memories of Froyle School are from 1934 until I left at Easter 1941 to take up employment with Messrs Courage and Co., Brewers of Alton.

I remember the summers when, on our way to school, we would pop the bubbles of tar in the road where it had been poured to fill the pot holes and we would get ourselves covered with tar. It would get all over us, particularly in our hair. Many children took their mid-day snack to school where it was not practical to walk home and back in the lunchtime. I well remember taking a 'screw' of cocoa (a mixture of cocoa and sugar in a piece of paper, twisted at the top) and being able to make a hot drink by adding part of the $^1/_3$ of a pint of 'school milk'. This milk was not free as is often believed and a payment of 2½ pence was made on Monday morning, representing ½ pence per third of a pint Monday to Friday inclusive. The hot water came from the large cast iron kettles which were kept on the stove top in each classroom. The idea behind this was that a constantly steaming kettle would be good for the children's breathing. Also on Monday morning Mrs Bygrave would collect the contributions for 'the School Outing'. This was

Jack Cooper, standing, and Basil Lee cruising on the River Wey near Mill Court in 1937

accumulated until the Summer when the whole school, and their families, went by coach to the sea-side, usually Hayling Island 'because the water is shallow there and it's safer for the children!'. The other annual trip was to The Aldershot Tattoo where we patriotically cheered the khaki-clad soldiers in Rushmoor Area and booed the 'Fuzzie-Wuzzies', uncaring that they always lost and were really soldiers with black faces anyway.

Holidays remained more or less as described, the important one being 'Oppin Olidays' when most families made enough money to see them through the Winter. The school staff were often employed as Tallymen but not, as some would have it, that they were the only ones who could add up and write! Half day holidays were few and far between. What is now Religious Instruction was then known as 'Scriptures' and was taught first thing each morning and on Wednesdays the Vicar, The Reverend Father Sangster, known in the playground as 'Daddy', would come in. Each year the Scripture Inspector would come and woe betide anyone who didn't know the answers. The exam usually finished mid-morning and at the end the Inspector who, I suspect was really a very nice man, would have us on the edge of our seats waiting for the usual 'Well, you all know that I can give you a half-day holiday if I think you have done well in the exam'. A long pause would follow ..... Every eye was fixed on him. We waited. He would turn to 'Tommy' Knight and say 'What do you think, Headmaster?' One could almost hear the silent prayers rising. 'Well, it's really up to you, Inspector'. Another long pause .... 'Yes, I think they should have a half-day'. The sighs of relief were audible and with a 'Thank you' we were off for the rest of the day. Another notable day was when the piano tuner came. Teaching was not possible during the tuning and we were given reading or drawing. Someone was always elected to ask, at the end of the session, if the piano tuner would play a tune for us. He always did and it was always a number called 'The Cuckoo'. We later found out that was the only tune he could play!

As I look back on those school days, I can hear Mrs Bygrave saying yet again, 'You are the worst writer in the school. I showed your composition (there were no essays in those days!) to Mr Bygrave and he said that no-one who wrote that badly could possibly be going to Froyle school. You will do one hundred lines of pot-hooks and hangers'. It was the ultimate shame to have ones work 'shown to Mr Bygrave'. Pot-hooks and hangers were f, g, h, j, b, etc. And I can remember Mr Knight's final advice on leaving school - 'Always tell the truth - you don't have to remember what you said'."

No doubt these will bring back many memories to those pupils who were at school at the same time and, probably, not all those memories will be happy ones! One 'youngster', now in his late 70s, remembers that the boys used to chew up blotting paper and flick it onto the ceiling with rulers. Mr Knight couldn't work out what the strange noise was, whenever his back was turned. Eventually he found out and every one of the perpetrators received the cane and had to spend hours cleaning the high ceiling of the schoolroom until there wasn't a trace of blotting paper left!

Another 'lad' remembers being caught, pulling the hair of the girl sitting in front of him. He was called up to Mr Knight's desk and received three lashes of the cane on each hand. Another child made him laugh, so another three lashes were dealt out. He was then locked in the schoolroom after class to write out 500 times, "I must not pull young girls' hair". Apparently Mr Knight forgot to come back and let the youngster out, so when it got dark he had to climb out of the window and walk home! Now, this story may have gained a little embellishment in the telling over some seventy years, but there is no doubting the fact that Mr Knight was a strict teacher - and yet his pupils loved and respected him, which says a great deal!

Mary Cranstone, nee Stevens (1938-1945), also recalls that Mr Knight was strict and would often use the cane on very naughty boys. "I remember some who, when they knew they were in trouble, rubbed orange peel on their hands so the cane would split. Mrs Bygrave was very fond of rapping our knuckes with a ruler. I was quite often rapped for talking in class! When I first started school I was on the small side and Mrs Bygrave said she would like to put me in a shoe box in Whites Window in Aldershot. Miss Pullinger, the Infant teacher, was very kind to us. On very cold mornings she would warm our milk on the coke burning stove which was used to heat the classroom. I enjoyed my days at Froyle - it had great character and played an essential part in village life."

A final anecdote from this decade comes from Maureen Fry, nee Chappell (1940-1946). She recalls that, amongst the collection of memorabilia in Mr Knight's 'museum' was a German helmet and a coconut. The senior boys always had their lunch in Mr Knight's classroom and on one particular day her brother, Bert, put the helmet on while George Pritchard took aim at it with the coconut. Unfortunately Bert was sitting near the stove and the coconut missed the helmet and hit the iron kettle full of hot water simmering there, knocking it over Bert and badly scalding his leg.

Just as education seemed to begin to make strides again, the storm clouds of the Second World War began to gather, making the next decade a troubled one. However for a few more years the school continued quietly. The garden was pronounced a 'Grade A Garden' in 1938, so the Froyle boys would be well prepared to take part in the wartime 'Dig for Victory' Campaign!

The War Years

*Bob White (pushing) and Francis Milne doing their bit
for the war effort by collecting waste paper*

The Summer holiday of 1939 was divided into two parts; the first, for corn harvest, was from August 4th - 14th and on the children's return to school they were told to take their gas masks with them. These masks had been supplied by local wardens a few weeks earlier as another war now seemed inevitable.

"The children have been asked to bring their gas masks to school this week, for practice and adjustment. Two parents refused to allow the children to bring their masks." (August 21st 1939)

"Four gas masks have been found to be faulty or the wrong size." (August 22nd 1939)

These problems were reported to Froyle's own Air Raid Wardens who had been training in wartime procedures for some months. The gas masks were supplied in strong cardboard boxes with a string shoulder strap, although some children used ready-made bags and cases instead, mostly made from rexine, a 'leather-look' cloth.

*Pam, Reg and Beryl Vivian and their friend Rosemary Fittock
with their gas masks in 1940, outside the Vivian's butchers shop*

During the course of the war, the masks had to be taken everywhere with their owners and children were sent home to collect theirs if forgotten. Thankfully they were never needed to be put into actual use but after the use of poisonous gas by the Germans in the First War, there was a great fear, especially in the first year of the war, that gas might be a lethal weapon again and gas mask practice became as regular an event as fire practice. The masks were manufactured from light sheets of strong flexible rubber; they had a pig-like filter or snout and a clear oval eye-screen and they were fitted to the head shape by adjustable straps.

Jack Cooper remembers being fitted for his mask, "They were in cardboard cartons with long strings. My hair kept getting tangled in the buckles at the back!"

Because School closed again on August 25th - this time for the hop harvest - there is no mention of the actual outbreak of war in the log book. But it is a date which few will ever forget. At 11.15 a.m. on that fateful Sunday morning of September 3rd 1939, Prime Minister Neville Chamberlain was heard to declare over the radio, "This morning the British Ambassador in Berlin handed the German Government a final note stating that unless we heard from them by 11 o'clock that they were prepared at once to withdraw their troops from Poland a state of war would exist between us. I have to tell you now that no such undertaking has been received, and that consequently this country is at war with Germany."

Almost before he had finished speaking the first air-raid siren was sounded - a false alarm, as it happened - and Britain was at war with Germany. The evacuation of children from vulnerable areas had already begun on 1st September and during the next few days 827,000 schoolchildren, 524,000 mothers with pre-school children, 13,000 expectant mothers and 173,000 others were evacuated across the country. But as the feared air-raids failed to materialise, a steady drift back of population followed, amounting to 80 percent of the original total by 1940. However, the Blitz in the summer and autumn of that year led to a new wave of evacuation, with nearly 1,400,000 evacuees recorded by early 1941. This was to be followed by a final exodus in 1944 under the new threat of the V1 and V2 flying bombs.

In Froyle there is no mention in the log books of any evacuees, which is not really surprising when one considers the proximity of Lasham, Odiham, Bordon and Aldershot. However, people can remember children attending school with names like Harry and Jimmy Short, Heather and Rosemary Fittock, Derek Murfin, Rita and Barbara Woodhouse, Muriel and Mildred Parrott, Joy and Pat Target, Basil Cumpstey, D. Eldridge. Jack Cooper remembers one of the Target children, ".....a girl named Target who came from London and, in the considered view of the boys in school, 'was a nice piece of stuff but talked all funny'."

Some other of the evacuees who made Froyle their home during the war years only recently returned for a Village Reunion.

Dorothy Salway, nee Diaper, pictured above, right, tells us how she and her family came to Froyle.

"I came from Portsmouth and the memory I will never forget is of the night we were in a large public shelter when Portsmouth was blitzed and we had to come out of the shelter and make our way to the bus station and wait for buses to take us out of the city. Everywhere was red and burning and we were not allowed to go into our houses in case of unexploded bombs. I remember being very upset because I had a much loved dog and we couldn't go in for him. As it happened he was OK, but later had to be destroyed, because we couldn't have him in the accommodation we were given in the Vicarage in Froyle. We were sent to places called 'Rest Centres' initially and then found accommodation a bit later. As I was just a young child I guess I settled in OK in Froyle and at the school as children accept things more than adults, I believe. I know it seemed very quiet in the village after being in the town. I have mostly pleasant memories of the time I spent at the school and remember Miss Pullinger being very nice and gentle when I started there. I grew to love the countryside and wasn't too keen to return to the town at first, whereas I believe my parents were rather happy to return."

Pat Milne remembers the evacuees well. Today, as Pat Pritchard, and also pictured opposite, seated, she looks back on her first days at Froyle School.

"I started school in the summer of 1939 at the age of 5 years, walking the mile from home with my mother on day one, but with my brother and a group of children living nearby after that first day. I went into the Infant class taught by Miss Pullinger, a middle aged lady with long dark brown hair, parted in the middle and plaited and twisted into trumpets around her ears. She wore thick stockings and skirts and twinsets always and I don't remember ever seeing her wearing any jewellery. She was quietly spoken and had a gentle manner and I liked her. After a few weeks war was declared, so we had to take a gas mask over one shoulder and dinner bag over the other to school every day. The local policeman, P.C. May, who was stationed in nearby Bentley, came to school and tried to emphasise the importance of carrying the gas mask at all times. I don't think we really ever realized the seriousness of the war and, on one occasion, we were seen wearing our gas masks to pass a property where the owners were boiling up their pig food and the stench was horrible. We were reported to P.C. May and he made us stand in front of the class and told us off. The boys had to write lines to the effect that gas masks were not toys, but I was OK because I was only five! In the early 40s the staff room was turned into a kitchen and Mrs

David Brownjohn (wearing cap) with two evacuees who stayed at his family's home

Whittock was employed as cook and school dinners were introduced. Around the same time the evacuees arrived in Froyle from Portsmouth increasing the school numbers to over 100. The next two years were the best at primary school as the evacuees joined in everything, both at school and outside, and the feeling was of everyone working together. The parents helped in the kitchen with preparing dinners, the children went picking blackberries and Mr Knight's apples to have for puddings, and all vegetables from the allotments and local gardens were used - nothing was wasted, and the school dinners cost the princely sum of 2s/6d a week!"

Dorothy Diaper's mother, Marian, worked as a dinner lady at the school and Dorothy recalls just how good those dinners used to be, "My mother and

Mrs Whittock were both good cooks and I still remember the minced meat in lovely thick gravy and the super chocolate puddings and custard. School dinners were something to look forward to then!"

School meals at Froyle began in 1944 and each day during the first month, 44 dinners were served. Many of the mothers of the children were now at work so the tradition of 'going home to dinner' changed and the children were supervised by the teachers, the cook and kitchen helper.

School dinners were challenging for the cook, to say the least, with food rationing having been introduced on the 8th January 1940. Every man, woman and child was issued with a ration book. This rationing took five principal forms: Simple, ordinary rationing of certain basic foods: sugar, meat, fats, bacon, tea, cheese. Points rationing for tinned goods, dried fruit, cereals and pulses, syrup and treacle, biscuits etc. Group rationing, where the total amount could be taken in one of several commodities, e.g. jam and other preserves.

Distribution of a number of important foods (e.g. milk, dried milk, eggs, dried eggs and oranges) was controlled to ensure that priority allowances were made available for those who needed them most, e.g. babies, expectant mothers, and invalids. Rationing of sweets began on 26th July 1942. The general ration book contained two pages of personal points to be used solely for obtaining sweets.

On the whole, as there were no staff changes due to conscription etc., school proceeded fairly normally apart from having buckets of sand and stirrup pumps on view and sticky brown paper strips on the windows, to prevent the glass shattering from blast. Arrangements must have been made for taking shelter in an air raid and traces of wooden battens on the Junior classroom window, plus old blackout curtains discovered years later in the 'cubbyhole', suggest that at least one room could be blacked out and used after dark, provided of course not a chink of light showed through!

Jack Cooper remembers that, "the school windows were all taped up and classes finished earlier in the winter to get us all home before the air raids started."

Maureen Chappell recalls, "During the war, when there was a threat of machine gunning from German aeroplanes, Mr Knight divided the children up by where they lived and told us to walk on opposite sides of the road. Those from the Prince of Wales end walked in single file on the right. Those around the Methodist Church, i.e. the Milnes, Vasts, Shillings and Chappells, walked on the left. Husseys Pond end joined the road at the Beeches and walked on the right. This was a habit I have never got out of. Even today, when I walk to Upper Froyle, I always walk on the wrong side of the road."

He continues, "When we got home from school one of our treats was to collect enough money to buy a loaf from the Post Office and divide it between us. Although sugar, fat, etc was rationed, at that time flour wasn't. The crust of a fresh cottage loaf was wonderful."

Weather conditions were quite severe during the first winter of the war and, after the fortnight's Christmas holiday, an epidemic of measles broke out and lasted the whole of the Spring Term. Things improved with warmer weather after Easter but, as the fear of invasion grew, the Whitsun holiday was restricted to three days and the Summer holiday to two weeks. As most children still worked in the hopfields in the late summer, *"registers were not to be marked until mid-September"* and even then only 31 out of 73 pupils on the books were present! September passed and with it the Battle of Britain. By this time the pupils were becoming skilled at recognising aircraft, both 'theirs' and 'ours', particularly if they were out working in the fields. Pat Milne's brother, Francis (1935-1941), remembers standing in a hop field and watching the actual Battle taking place in the skies above him.

The first mention of enemy action in Froyle School's log book was on October 1st 1940, when Mr Knight wrote,

"closing of registers delayed as many children were late owing to Air Raid during the night."

Morale was kept high by the singing of patriotic songs. Jack Cooper recalls, "Mr. Knight felt that the older children should learn our Allies' National Anthems. I remember learning the English words to the French National Anthem and singing them in class."

Winter school hours were changed, the start and finish being delayed half an hour from 9.00 to 9.30 a.m. and 3.30 to 4.00 p.m., probably due to the clocks not being changed from Summer time that Autumn. In the very wet Spring of 1941 the timetable was often re-arranged to fit in gardening on fine days. In April that year the boys were taken over to the Park to gather sheep's wool from the fences and hedges. Flocks of sheep were increased to help with the food shortage, much lamb having come from New Zealand in refrigerated ships pre-war. The girls were encouraged to knit gloves and balaclava helmets for the troops and blanket squares for hospitals. There was a shortage of stock supplies for schools, particularly paper, and pupils' exercise books were inspected regularly to make sure no space was wasted. Pencils were also in short supply and had to be used down to the last half inch, special holders being provided to enable this. The children took pride in seeing who could make their pencils last the longest. New textbooks were scarce, and wartime books were printed on low quality paper to a special wartime standard.

Encouraged by the 'Make Do and Mend' Campaign to save new materials, in needlework lessons the girls learnt how to turn old garments into new, smaller ones and, later in the war, parachute silk was also used. Pat Milne has rather unpleasant memories of those days, "Mrs Bygrave made me darn her husband's clothes. I didn't like her. She had favourites and I wasn't one of them." Marion Allen, nee Beckhurst (1940-1951), was always getting into trouble with Mrs Bygrave, "I was always singing - not in class - but at break times - and this seemed to annoy her." Although undoubtedly Mrs Bygrave achieved good results in both academic and creative work, she was not the most popular of Froyle's teachers. Francis Milne's unhappiest memory was, "being rapped over the knuckles by Mrs Bygrave because I cut the heads off a bunch of flowers one of the girls was taking to the teacher.", and Joan Ezzard (1945-51) also remembers Mrs Bygrave caning her over the back of her hand for very little.

In the autumn of 1941 boys were allowed to go for a day's potato picking and nine boys took advantage of a day off school, plus some payment for the task. How often this happened we are not sure, but Pat Milne recollects that one group of lads went to pick potatoes for Mr Andrew who farmed in Upper Froyle. At the end of the day when the tractor arrived in the field expecting to take several sacks of potatoes to the farm, it was discovered the boys had only managed to pick a bucket full each. They were not encouraged to go again!

Women now filled many jobs as men were in the armed forces or doing essential work. This meant women caretakers in school with Mrs Lucas taking over her husband's duties in November 1940. However, in December 1941, when her child had whooping cough, the teachers were left to clean out and light the stoves, also sweep and dust the classrooms.

The 'Milk in Schools' scheme commenced in 1941 and Froyle School children were supplied with a third of a pint of free milk from Mr Andrew. In April 1942 the Easter holiday was for three weeks, to include a potato planting holiday. Empire Day was now a very important celebration with patriotic messages read and suitable songs sung. Sometimes visitors came to speak to the children and gave prizes for essays after their talks. P.C.May took Road Safety sessions during the war, also lessons on various 'dangers', wartime and otherwise presumably! Gas mask drill continued, with the log book recording a practice at the school in July 1943.

Attendances were low in the snowy winter in January 1945 when only 18 children out of a possible 59 attended school, the log book recorded,

> "More snow during the night. Many of the children have no suitable boots, the parents have the money in many cases, but no coupons. Also suitable boots are in short supply in the shops."
>
> *(January 30th 1945)*

Wellington boots were not made during the war as the rubber materials were scarce and required for military purposes.

Termly exams were still given to the children and classes were re-arranged at the beginning of the Summer Term each year.

Victory came at last and the entries in the log book for May 8th and 9th 1945 were made in red ink - they really were Red Letter Days! There was no school on the two V.E. Days. All over the country, parties were arranged, in schools or in streets with fancy dress and flags flying. Two days school holiday were also given for V.J. Day on 15th and 16th August, as the school had not broken up like most schools in the country because of the late hop-harvest. One other day's holiday at that same time was on July 5th as a polling station for the General Election was in the school buildings.

During the Second World War the loss of husbands and sons from families in Froyle was much less than in the previous one. The names of Hubert Brownjohn, C.Goodyear, R.S.Morgan, W.A.Morris and W.Stevens were added to the War Memorial, together with those of Richard Chubb, who was killed in an air raid in 1944 while on civilian war service in London, and Phyllis Savage, whose death, in 1946, was due to an accident at her WAAF camp.

The most important educational event of the decade was R.A.Butler's 1944 Education Act which was to affect all schools, which were now divided into Primary (up to 11) and Secondary (11 to 15 +).

This meant that at 11 + in the future all children would leave their school to go to a bigger area secondary school - in Alton to Eggars Grammar School or Alton Senior School, but in some areas there were also Technical Schools. This would reduce the numbers of children in village schools and Froyle numbers dropped to just above 40 by 1946.

The 'Scholarship' exam was abolished, selection would now be by assessment plus an I.Q. test. Primary schools became 'County' (state) or 'Controlled' or 'Aided' schools (church) according to how much help they received from the local education authority. New methods were recommended involving the experience, curiosity and interest of the children and project or topic work was encouraged.

With the raising of the school leaving age teachers were again in short supply so many 'Emergency' Training Colleges were set up by the Ministry of Education and many 'demobbed' service personnel and others, sometimes older, took a shortened condensed teaching course of one year, instead of the usual two.

Maureen Chappell was one of those children who passed the 11 + exam and, as a treat for doing so well, Mrs Bygrave invited her and the others who had passed to her home in Aldershot. "She took us to the pictures." Maureen said, "The film we saw was called 'The Lives of the Bengal Lancers'. I think she thought it would be educational!"

We believe the school group above was photographed in 1946.

Back row, left to right: May Hopkins, Betty Cooper, ? Cumpsty, Alberta Harris, Mable Emery, Heather Beckhurst
Third row: John Cooper, ? , Raymond Fry, Harry Naylor, George Scott, David Heath, ? , Gerald Fry, ? Booth, Derek Whittock, Denis Worsfold, Kenneth Tab, John Sommers
Second row: June Scott, Pauline Rhodes, ? Cumpsty, Shirley Goodyear, Anita Sommers, Lena Booth, Eileen Parrack, Marie Bennett, Violet Lucas, Pauline Hopkins, Joan Ezzard, Kathleen Smith
Front row: Chris Pritchard, Ian Cottrell, ? , ? Wells, Kenny Emery

April 18th, 1946 marked the end of an era when Mr Knight wrote in the log book,

> *"At the end of the Easter Holidays, May 4th, I cease to be Headmaster, as I am retiring, so this is my last day of actual teaching. Mrs J.A.Bygrave has been appointed Head Mistress and all the 11+ children will go to Alton Modern Secondary School."*

A Time of Celebration

'Flower Fairies' in the late 1940s

So, some twenty four years after first arriving, Mrs Jesse Bygrave became Headmistress, the first woman to take on the role at Froyle School. In January 1947 there were some petty thefts at the school, so P.C.May visited and spoke on 'Honesty and Dishonesty', at the same time returning a pair of gloves which had been stolen two days earlier!

At this stage, anthracite and coal were still required for the school stove and fires. The cesspit also had to be emptied frequently and a supply of 'dry earth' was constantly required for the 'bucket' toilets, probably Elsan type by this stage. The H.M.I. report for 1947 commended both the children's work and their behaviour. Mrs Bygrave was also praised for her useful system of recording each pupil's progress; as also was the work of her assistant, Miss Pullinger, both having given over 25 years service to the school. The high standard of needlework and the school meals provided were also commented upon.

"Copy of Report dated 15ᵗʰ April 1947.

Inspected on 5ᵗʰ February 1947.

The present Head Mistress of this Junior Mixed and Infant School and her assistant have worked together here for nearly twenty-five years. The previous Head Master, under whom they both served, retired nine months ago.

The Infants Class is well managed by the Supplementary teacher. Unfortunately they have to sit in old-fashioned desks, but there is a large room available for this activity. Reading and Number are both well advanced. The singing of nursery rhymes would be improved if more careful attention were given to the words. Some new reading primers would be a useful addition to the equipment.

In Class 1 there is good progress in the 9 to 10 years age group.

Arithmetic methods are practical, and mental work is quick. Reading is clear and the expression good. A high standard of neatness is achieved in the written work. Perhaps the poems, which are memorised, might be shorter.

The tone of this school is extremely good. The pupils are very well behaved and most courteous to their teachers. They respond politely when questioned and work quietly. All the work done is very thorough, and the standard quite high in view of the migratory population from which the school suffers.

The Head Mistress devotes much thought to the whole curriculum and has a useful system of recording each pupil's progress. Experiment might be made with free expression work in the teaching of Art. Teaching methods are up to date and the schemes are sensibly planned.

The especial interest of the Head Mistress is in Needlework and in the past there have been conspicuous successes in National Needlecraft Competitions. The work being done by the present Junior girls is of a high standard.

A good school meal is cooked on the premises and eaten in the Infants Classroom. There is practically 100 per cent attendance.

Staff Mrs J.A.Bygrave, Head Mistress, and Miss M. Pullinger."

The year drew to a close with a day's holiday to celebrate the wedding of Princess Elizabeth to Prince Philip.

By 1948 the country had begun to recover from the effects of the six years of war. The armed forces had all been demobbed and family life restored. There was a change from the life of the 30s, when villages were more isolated. Many people had moved about and met different types of people during the war and society had begun to break down class barriers.

Following the implementation of the 1944 Education Act, life in primary schools was gradually changing, with the introduction of more freedom of choice. It was to be 'child-centred', children experimenting with new ideas as individuals or in groups, instead of the formal classroom education with the teacher doing all the talking and with a great use of text books which children read round the class. Change was slower in percolating through to the more rural areas and where the staff were older and more set in their ways, but newly trained teachers were keen to try out their ideas - not all of which were always successful!

Froyle School continued with the same staff and in the same way as it had done during the war years. Empire Days and Armistice Day were still important celebrations and for the next few years talks on 'The Empire', 'The Growth of the Empire' and 'Empire Building', were given by visitors to the school. However, with the decline of the Empire, the independence of many states and the formation of the 'Commonwealth', May 24th was no longer celebrated as Empire Day and was replaced with a day in March called 'Commonwealth Day'.

In the Summer of 1948 mention is made of the kitchen water heater needing attention, the kitchen drain being blocked and an accident to the cook when she inadvertently dropped a pile of plates on her foot, bruising it badly; there was a lot of illness and temporary help in the kitchen that term. The health of the canteen staff was of paramount importance and they were not allowed to work if there was any infection in their homes. If temporary help was not available the teachers sometimes had to cook or prepare the children's dinners. Most of the children now stayed in school over the dinner time and sandwiches were discouraged.

In the Autumn Term the large classroom was redecorated by a local firm and surplus furniture from it was returned to the store at Winchester, as numbers

School group 1948

School group 1950

were falling and smaller numbers of desks etc. were needed. The Vicar came in regularly to talk to the children and once presented them with a picture of 'the Child in the Temple' - modern art had not yet penetrated the school, so the pictures on the walls would have been very traditional and possibly uninspiring!

There were the usual accidents to various children, one was recorded as having been pushed home on the Headmistress's bicycle! Mrs Bygrave suffered some eye trouble at this time, until she was fitted with contact lenses - a very modern innovation! Children's eyesight was regularly tested but most of those needing them wore the regulation round ugly glasses supplied cheaply by the authorities.

Traditionally, the Headteacher gave the children a party every Christmas and this was thoroughly enjoyed by everyone. In later years the event would be taken over by parents. Every summer there was a school outing to Hayling Island by coach, but there were not many other excursions.

The school was visited regularly by the doctor and nurse, the dentist and other specialists to check the children's eyesight, hearing, speech etc. and occasionally the educational psychologist was called in to see children with emotional problems. H.M.I.s visited the school and also an increasing number of advisers in specialist subjects. Infectious diseases were treated very seriously, with immunisation for diphtheria and polio, swabs taken for scarlet fever and checks made on likely contacts or carriers by the Alton Isolation Hospital. The first aid box was to be clearly visible, but still only contained very basic supplies such as iodine and 'acriflavine' and sterile containers and dishes, scissors and safety pins. The village doctor was contacted if the extent of injury was unknown, but the children had to go to Alton if an X-ray was required.

By 1950 there was another General Election and the new government was to introduce a 'National Health' scheme with free treatment for everyone, unless they wished to be privately treated. There was more scope for Mrs Bygrave in spending money; more petty cash was provided for the school kitchen as vegetables sometimes had to be purchased locally, although most of the food was delivered in bulk by the county contractors. Now that the school had 'Controlled' status as a church school, the church had less authority over its organisation and teaching; Ascension Day, which for years had been celebrated by a church service followed by a day's holiday, was now to be an ordinary school day with the older children attending a brief service in church at the beginning of the day.

There was still no wireless belonging to the school but one was occasionally borrowed or brought in and in May 1951 the children listened to a broadcast by King George VI at the opening of the 'Festival of Britain' celebrations, which were planned to show off to the world what Britain could do and make now that the war was over. Numbers of children in the school began to grow with 61 on the books in the Autumn Term 1951.

School group 1951

School group 1953

Schools in the area were closed from October 12th to October 22nd 1951 as army manoeuvres were being held locally and the school was closed again on October 25th for another election, so it was quite a disrupted term for the staff.

At the beginning of 1952 everyone was shocked and saddened by the sudden death of King George VI and a service was held in the church in memory of the King, the older children attending - this was followed by a two minute silence in school afterwards. People began to look forward to the reign of a new Queen as Princess Elizabeth had succeeded her father but was not actually crowned until the following year.

Health Education took on greater importance in the fifties; a new First Aid box was supplied in the Autumn Term. These boxes were made of metal, painted black, with a red cross on the lid; they still contained only basic requirements, such as bandages, scissors, an enamel bowl, cotton wool, tweezers and iodine and antiseptics. 28lbs of carbolic soap were delivered the same term, so there must have been a very 'healthy' smell around the school!

The kitchen was now quite an important part of the school. Deliveries of stock and supplies were duly recorded, but the cook was in control of the kitchen and her permission must be obtained for others to go into it. Various people from the village were brought in to help out when the cook or the kitchen helper was absent. Plates, tea towels and check gingham for tablecloths were replaced when necessary. There were occasionally requests for free meals by parents in financial difficulties and, although names of these children were not disclosed, it was fairly obvious each Monday morning when the week's dinner money was collected, a task undertaken by the teachers until 1957, when the first clerical assistant for the school actually commenced work.

The School Meals Service was regarded as a great success nationwide, producing healthier children and encouraging better behaviour, particularly when children and teachers ate together in small groups. The food was typical 1950s fare - meat and two veg, macaroni cheese, fish on Fridays and always a cooked dessert such as rice pudding, semolina, tapioca or jam sponge and custard. Shirley Parker, nee Pritchard, (1948-1954) had only very happy memories of her lunches there, "School dinners were good, cooked by Mrs Whittock and Mrs Binfield." and Sally Johnson, nee Bennett, (1952-1959) also remembered the culinary delights served up by these particular ladies.

Perhaps these children remembered their school lunches with such delight because, at the time of the Queen's Accession in 1952, Britain was a country struggling with the aftermath of the Second World War. Sugar, butter, cheese, margarine, cooking fat, bacon, meat and tea were all still rationed and many other foods were also in short supply. For many children, school dinners were, perhaps, the best meals they had! Rationing slowly came to an end; bread in July 1948 (this was only rationed on the 21st July 1946); jam in December 1948;

School group 1953

School group 1953

clothes in March 1949 and petrol in May 1950. Tea was de-rationed in October 1952; sweets in February 1953; eggs in March 1953 and cream in April 1953. In celebration of the Queen's Accession to the throne, everyone was allowed an extra 1 lb of sugar and 4 oz of margarine for Coronation month. Sugar was de-rationed in September 1953; butter, cheese, margarine and cooking fats in May 1954; and finally, meat in June 1954. In November 1952 the poppies, annually sold in the school to help disabled ex- servicemen, were made into a wreath to be placed on the War Memorial at 'The Beeches' on November 11th.

With 79 children at school at the beginning of 1953, an extra teaching assistant was requested from the County, but an offer of clerical assistant was not taken up. A post of assistant teacher was advertised in February 1953 but the lady interviewed decided, on reflection, not to take up the post after consultation with Winchester. There was still no proper staffroom in the school and the conditions probably deterred some people from teaching in the village, also transport, although better than pre-war, was not always easy. Mr Knight, having retired as Headmaster, became the correspondent to the managers and was called into school when support was needed, such as when Mrs Bygrave received a telephone call from the police informing her that boys had broken into an empty cottage in the village, or when she telephoned the police because an irate grandparent would not leave the school premises. A letter of apology was later received from the boy's mother! It is not known exactly when a school telephone had been installed.

The Queen's Coronation was held on June 2nd and there was a school holiday with at least some of the children being lucky enough to watch the ceremony on their TV sets at home. On the Saturday, June 6th, a party was held in school, arrangements having been previously made with the chairman of the managers, Col.Newton Davis. The Froyle Scrapbook, compiled by the village's W.I. group for a competition in 1952, records the events of that exciting week,

"In the evening of Coronation Day, in spite of the cold and rather damp drizzle, a cheerful crowd gathered in the recreation ground to light a glorious bonfire, the leaping flames of which must have been seen many miles away.

On Saturday, June 6th the children had a Tea at the School. A conjurer entertained them after tea and then everyone went into Mr Andrew's field for sports, and a Maypole Dance, charmingly danced by the boys and girls of Froyle School, trained by Mrs Bygrave.

Later earth from the small hands of Froyle schoolchildren helped to plant flowering trees to commemorate the Coronation at Froyle Recreation Ground. Seven year old Elizabeth Ottley and ten year old Brian Hankin planted two (of the nine) trees near the entrance of the ground. All the children filed past to throw a handful of earth round the trees. Lt.Col.C.Newton-Davis, chairman of Froyle Parish Council, said that the children were asked to help in the ceremony as it was hoped that the trees would be in their care... In his hands lay the selection of trees, which included flowering Japanese cherry and crab trees, purple plum and an August-flowering Indian bean tree."

At the end of the Summer Term, Miss Pullinger retired, after thirty one years of teaching the Infant Class. There is no mention of any special presentations, but surely there must have been one. Much to our regret, we have no photographs of her at all, but she is remembered by all those who were taught by her as a quiet, kind person, who always dressed in green and wore her hair in plaits rolled up into 'earphones'. Almost every ex-pupil had happy memories of their time in her Infant class. Comments were, "She didn't tell me off", "She was popular with everyone", and, "She always had time to listen".

During this time there were the usual everyday school crises,

> *"Robert Barnes in Class I was withdrawn from school just after 10 a.m. when the Head Teacher learned that on the previous evening he had swallowed a large button (1 inch diameter) from his raincoat and of which his parents had no knowledge. The boy is to stay at home as a precautionary measure."*   *(April 1953)*

> *"John Peters was swinging on the desk when he fell and cut the outer part of his ear.... he had three stitches."*   *(September 1954)*

Two temporary teachers came to the school in September, another was interviewed and offered Miss Pullinger's post in November 1953, but resigned a few months later. By now numbers on roll had increased to 80 and two temporary supply teachers were appointed, Mrs E.Worsfold and Mrs H.Robinson. Mrs M.Eddington was appointed assistant teacher on November 23rd, but did not appear to see eye to eye with Mrs Bygrave and left the following Spring.

In March 1954 the caretaker left suddenly and various supply teachers still came into school but it was not until the Autumn Term of 1954 that Mrs Cawthorn took over the Infant class, only to leave again in December as her husband had been moved out of the area. The school roof was discovered to be in need of repair that Autumn and the piano needed a general overhaul. A new school cupboard was delivered, the old ones mostly having been on the premises since the school was opened in 1868.

The H.M.I. report of June, 1955, was again very favourable, commending the teachers for the children's standard of work and praised them particularly for their efforts in a difficult period of growing numbers and difficulty in obtaining teachers!

> *"This school has more than doubled its numbers since the last report in 1947. There are now 85 children on roll. There are two playgrounds, each containing some pleasant trees, but the surface is uneven, loose and, in winter, muddy. The fence between the School and the School*

House is in a very dilapidated condition. The three classrooms are of good size; the largest, containing the piano, is used for Assembly and when the playground is unfit for use, for Physical Education.

The Infant's classroom is used as a dining room, the school meal is cooked in a small kitchen on the premises, the attendance for the meal is nearly 100%. The Offices consist of buckets. In a classroom there is a sink with running water, but wash basins are of the portable type.......

Every care is taken by the teachers to give these children a happy school-life, and to teach them to behave courteously to others; the children's ready response reflects credit on all concerned.

Staff:- Mrs J.A.Bygrave, Mrs B.Roberts, Mrs Grey."

Mrs Grey had taken over the Infant class in the Autumn of 1953, with Mrs Roberts joining the staff as Junior Assistant Teacher in January 1955.

Mrs Bygrave, on the right of the photograph, introduces Mr Heywood, the first Headteacher of the newly opened Lord Mayor Treloar College, to the children in 1955

With packaging of shop goods becoming more general, litter became a problem in the village so a talk was arranged in school on 'Litter in the Village'. Caretaking matters were discussed at the managers meeting that term and there was agreement that twenty two and a half hours per week were reasonable for the work involved, which involved dealing with 'bucket' sanitation, coal fires and stoves! The large classroom stove needed to be repaired so it was removed that September and all the chimneys were swept. September returns showed that 48 children were receiving school milk and 74 paid for school meals. More equipment was received for the kitchen and P.E. equipment arrived after a visit from the new P.E. Adviser. 'Letting' sheets, for school premises hire, school meal registers and summaries, also a 'furniture in school' report, were all forwarded to the County Education Officer in Winchester. The 'offices' were lime-washed and four new doormats were delivered. A request by the Roman Catholic Church in Alton for a day course to be held on the school premises was referred to the C.E.O. and there is no more mention of it after this. The C.E.O. was also consulted over the attendance of the children in church for Mass during school time, now that the school had become 'Controlled'.

In January 1956 numbers had risen to 82 - almost double the numbers in 1947. That month a pupil was knocked down by a car outside the school.

"An Infant boy, Trevor Cousins, aged 6, was this afternoon at 3.45 p.m. knocked down by a car approximately 150 yards from the school. He was taken to the Alton General Hospital by the Head Teacher for treatment.....he sustained a broken clavicle."   *(January 1956)*

Following the accident Mrs Bygrave wrote to Alton Secondary Modern School and requested that their school coach should not pick up scholars directly outside Froyle School as it was very dangerous on the bend there. In March the kitchen scales were exchanged following a routine check by the Inspector for Weights and Measures. A phone call was made to Alton railway station as supplies of soap sent by rail had not been delivered. The same month a refrigerator was supplied to the kitchen and a wardrobe cupboard was delivered for the use of kitchen staff. This had to be kept in the large classroom, until moved into the Infant cloakroom many years later. A fire blanket was sent for kitchen use. The annual outing in the summer was again to Hayling Island. Many North Hampshire children still rarely went to the seaside before the days of widespread car ownership and their only opportunity was on organised coach excursions such as this. Michael Ezzard (1952-1958) was just one youngster who remembered these trips as the highlight of the year, "I remember a day trip to Hayling Island with our names on little felt labels. Mine was yellow".

In the Autumn of 1956 a boy from the school was discovered to be working for a local farmer; both the parents and the farmer were cautioned about this, as it was illegal under the age of 14. When the correspondent visited Mrs Bygrave that term, the two of them decided that some clerical assistance would be useful particularly on Mondays, when dinner money was collected, recorded and paid in. So, in January 1957, Miss Bennett was appointed as the school's first clerical assistant, working part-time for 10 hours a week. By this time Mr Davis had replaced Mr Knight as correspondent to the managers. In November 1956 an Alresford firm installed electric light in the school and later in the month the supply was connected up by the Electricity Board. An electric fan was installed on the wall of the kitchen, to combat condensation and extract kitchen smells. During that winter, the dinner hour was again shortened, so that the children could go home at 3.30 p.m. in daylight. The Ascot heater in the kitchen was inspected as it was again not functioning properly - a common occurrence! Requests were made for more cupboards to house increasing stocks and some more modern desks, but these were not delivered until later in 1957. Roller towels were supplied for the school and the kitchen, also dusters and floorcloths. An infestation of mice was dealt with by the rodent officer, by putting down poison. Miss Ferguson, the County Adviser, visited the school in the Autumn Term to inspect the sanitation which was now causing concern. A visit from the County Auditors proved satisfactory.

This was to be the last term in school for Mrs Bygrave, who was retiring after a lifetime of service to the school. She was to be replaced by Mrs Joan Dean, who spent a Saturday in school to discuss organisation etc. Various County officials, including Mr Marsh, C.E.O., and the Music and Needlework Advisers, visited the school during the term to wish Mrs Bygrave well in her retirement. Her death, in the 60s, after a leg amputation, was recorded in the later log book.

This photograph, taken at the annual Village Fete in the Summer of 1957, shows Mrs Bygrave, having been presented with a bouquet by young Terry Penman

At her last 'Open Day' there was, of course, an exhibition of Needlework and Art & Craft and there was singing and dancing, her favourite subjects. The managers made her a presentation at the end of term and there was also a farewell service, followed by sports and teas. Many changes were about to overtake the school due to 'new brooms' and also the modern approach to education now developing. During the many years that Mrs Bygrave was in the school, the children's good standards were maintained and there appeared to be stability and a feeling of security for all who attended the school.

At the commencement of the Autumn Term 1957, when Mrs Dean took over the duties of Headteacher, there was a main change of staffing. Mrs Roberts was still teaching the younger Junior children but Miss Amabilino took charge of the Infant Class. Mrs Kelly visited the school once a week as a peripatetic headteacher relief teacher, enabling Mrs Dean to undertake many out of classroom duties, and Mrs Piggott became school secretary, a post later in the year to be filled by Mrs Tourell from Treloar College. Gerald (Gerry) Robinson (1953-1959) remembers the staff changes with some relief, "The most memorable event that sticks in my mind was the long overdue retirement of Mrs Bygraves and the appointment of Mrs Joan Dean as the new Headmistress. She was to take on the unenviable task of 'dragging' the old school out of the 'Dark Ages' and into the present day. And in her short stay there made an excellent job of doing just that. Mrs Dean came to the school at the same time as Miss Amabilino - it was like a breath of fresh air!"

The children began to go out of school more, on Nature Walks, or local visits to the hop yards or church, but they also ventured further afield to London to the Science Museum and to London Airport, in connection with their studies.

Attendance numbers fell rapidly during the first term as there was an influenza epidemic. On the worst day only 29 children out of 80 were present! During the year immunisations were given for poliomyelitis and diphtheria.

In school one innovation was the formation of a library, with a collection of books, borrowed and changed termly, from the County Library Mobile Schools Service. Meals changed to 'table service' with dishes containing meat and vegetables on each table as at home, in place of the meal queue waiting for the kitchen staff to dole out helpings onto a plate held by a child. Gingham tablecloths still covered the tables and it was even suggested by the County that flowers could decorate each table. Individual glasses and a water jug were also provided. A dining room assistant was appointed to supervise the children eating their meal. The old dining tables - long rectangular linoleum topped folding tables which warped when stacked in a high pile - were exchanged for new ones. These were formica topped semi hexagonal or octagonal tables which could be grouped together in various arrangements to suit the dinner room. Meals were still served in the Infant room at this time and this worried the newly appointed Infant Adviser, Miss Bradburn.

The School Meals Service was now sufficiently organised for a relief cook from Alton to come on temporary loan whilst the Froyle cook was ill. Meals served in school at this time were similar to those cooked at home, with a variety of meat and fish dishes and two vegetables every day, followed by quite exciting puddings.

A visitor from the County Architect's Department promised fresh lavatories, also cloakrooms with handbasins and drinking fountains in the near future. Colour schemes were also discussed:

> "Mr Moyle, Clerk of Works, came to discuss the repainting of the school. Colour schemes were chosen. Classroom 1 will be painted in yellows and sage greens; Classroom 2 in pinks and blues, with a red door; Classroom 3 in yellows and sage greens. Porches, corridor and office will also be sage greens and yellows. All woodwork will be light in colour."
> (May 1958)

Later on repairs to the roof and windows were carried out and the front wall was declared to be in a dangerous condition. A shed for P.E. equipment was ordered and erected later in the year, the P.E. Adviser having ordered better equipment for the school. A cupboard, which had fallen over and injured Mrs Robert's foot, was made secure and desk tops were re-surfaced, pending replacement by locker desks. School services were resumed in church for Harvest, Armistice, Christmas and Ascensiontide. The Reverend Tunks left the parish in 1958 and was presented with a book token by the children. Linda Woodward, nee Robinson (1955-1961), pictured below, standing far right, has an amusing memory about his association with the school. Apparently on one occasion, on his return from a trip abroad, he came round with ONE fresh pineapple for the whole school to share! The children were given one small chunk each!

Playing Rounders in the late 1950s

The new Vicar, Reverend Field, visited the school and expressed the wish to do some actual teaching. The number of visitors to the school increased considerably; apart from the regular visits from the school nurse, doctor, dentist, the welfare officer and H.M.I.s, the county advisers also visited, including new subject advisers. Headteachers' meetings took place termly in the area and once a year the school was closed for all the teachers to attend a refresher day course at Havant or in Winchester and, in later years, in Basingstoke. The pupils now had a 'Head Boy' and 'Head Girl'; school photographs were taken regularly; animals were encouraged to be kept in school to help with children's studies and two rabbits were given to the school by Mrs Smith, the licensee of the Prince of Wales public house in Lower Froyle. The school photographer called on June 26th 1958 to take a photograph of the whole school as well as class photographs.

Headteacher, Mrs Joan Dean, with her Upper Junior class of 1958

For Gerry Robinson, pictured above, front row, second right, one of his best memories of his time at Froyle School was the building of a climbing frame at the top of the playground. "This is where I spent a lot of my playtimes swinging from bar to bar, doing somersaults and hanging upside down. Needless to say, I fell off a few times! Mrs Dean brought in a cine camera and filmed me doing some stunts on the bars and showed it to the class with the kids sat on the floor in the central corridor with a screen on the door leading out into the playground." And what about a bad memory? "...the arrival of the school dental service. An old caravan equipped as a torture chamber used to park next door just over the wall in the grounds of the vicarage. I used to hate it !!"

Mrs Betty Roberts, with her Junior class of 1958

Miss Audrey Amabilino, with her Infant class of 1958

Froyle School in 1958

In bad weather the children were allowed to go home early, a procedure discontinued in later years because of safety regulations and the fact of many parents being out at work, so the children would have returned home to an empty house. There had been a complaint from the local police that school children were playing in the empty vicarage during the interregnum and parents were warned that prosecutions might follow! No doubt the youngsters were trying to see for themselves whether the tales of ghostly 'goings on' in the Vicarage were true or false. To this day, one particular bedroom of the house is said to be haunted and many local people tell of having heard strange noises there.

Preliminary meetings were held during the year to organise a P.T.A. in the school,

> *"A meeting of parents was held at school this evening. It was decided to form a parent-teacher association. A temporary committee was elected to plan initial meetings, consisting of Mrs Dean and Mrs Roberts - representing the staff, Mrs Robson, Mr Prosser and Mr Barnes, representing the parents and Miss Chubb representing the Managers."* (March 20th 1958)

And, a few months later,

> *"Parent-teacher association meeting....*
>
> *A permanent committee was elected, consisting of a Chairman/ Treasurer - Mrs Dean; Secretary - Mr Tourrell, with Mrs Roberts representing the teachers; Mr Barnes and Mrs Peters, the parents; Miss Chubb, the Managers."* (June 11th 1958)

110

There were the usual 'alarms and excursions' of school life - a boy with an eyelash in his eye was taken across to the sick bay at the Lord Mayor Treloar College where he was treated by the matron. This was the first actual mention in the log book of the new college which had recently opened up in the Froyle Place premises. The College catered for residential pupils with physical handicaps, as a follow up for work done at the Lord Mayor Treloar Orthopaedic Hospital in Alton, founded by Sir William Treloar in 1908. College grounds were offered for the use of football that year.

A more serious accident occurred later that year when an Infant boy on his way home, played on and pulled over on himself a workmen's hut. Luckily a parent who was nearby, rescued him and he was not seriously injured, although he was sent to hospital for treatment. The incident, as with all school accidents, was duly reported to the County on a special form with full details.

Children returning from the College after using its playing field facilities

The managers became concerned over the slowness in making the promised improvements to the school, Mrs Goschen sought the co-operation of the school for children to contribute in some way to the village fete and, in July, an Open Day was held combined with a Bring & Buy Sale to supplement school funds. The school year ended with an H.M.I. visit and closed for the normal summer holiday period. This was now the holiday school children have today - five weeks from the end of July until the beginning of September - no more split or staggered holidays for corn and hop harvests!

When the school re-assembled in September 1958, the interior had been redecorated in light colours. The County promised both toilets and heating by 1959, in the meantime a base was prepared for the vegetable store at the back of the kitchen. At the end of September it was announced that Mrs Dean would be leaving the school at the end of term to take up another headship appointment in Dorset. Mr W.(Bill) Lailey, the deputy head of Alton C of E School, would take over her duties the following January. In November Mr Lailey spent a day at Froyle School to become acquainted. Managers kept very much in touch with school affairs, meetings were held once a term after school and the managers were cooperative about consulting the authorities over the school improvements.

Education was considered a national priority in the post-war years and more money and materials were being constantly made available to improve conditions at state schools throughout the country, although one has to say that the money available rarely compared with the expectations of the schools! At an important P.T.A. meeting in October 1958, Mr Marsh, C.E.O., spoke to Froyle parents on 'Secondary Selection and Education in Hampshire'. There were visitors from Bentley, Long Sutton, Mayfield and Alton St.Lawrence Schools present that evening. In the second half of the term Mrs Dean and the older children worked with Miss Robertson the P.E. Adviser on combined art and movement studies, the work being shown to teachers from other schools and a film made. Visitors came to bid Mrs Dean 'goodbye' and a Farewell Christmas Party was held when she was presented with a book token. Although only at Froyle for two short years, Mrs Dean endeared herself to many of her pupils. Sally Bennett remembers saying 'farewell' to her as one of her most unhappy memories of her school days.

Dear Parent,

We proudly present this high class portrait at the very low price of five shillings per copy.

FURTHER COPIES. Including the original, three copies for fourteen shillings and sixpence. If the original enlargement is purchased, three postcard size copies may be obtained for 6/6.

In ordering further copies, please quote order number from back of photograph. Please remit all cash to School.

Assuring you of our best attention at all times.

B. M. & CO.
School Photographers
93 CHURCH ROAD,
HOVE,
SUSSEX

Richard Ezzard's first official school photograph - do you remember yours?

Rumours of Closure

Sharing secrets in the playground, 1962

For the next eight years the school was ably run by Mr William (Bill) Lailey, implementing the changes initiated by Mrs Dean and endeavouring to get the school completely modernised - in this respect the smaller rural schools were often somewhat behind their town counterparts.

Now retired and living with his wife in Milford-on-Sea, Mr Lailey remembers his days at Froyle School with affection,

"Little did I know that when I made my application in the Autumn Term of 1958 that I was about to enter a remarkably enjoyable period of my teaching life. At that time I was completing a ten year job as Deputy Head with a post of special responsibility for children with learning difficulties in a school of some three hundred pupils.

Froyle School was to become my first Headship position, and I took up my duties at commencement of the Spring Term 1959. There were 55 pupils on roll and two rabbits!

The school was staffed by Mrs Betty Roberts, Miss Audrey Amabilino and Mrs Kelly, a peripatetic teacher who attended one day a week to relieve the head teacher of teaching duties. Mrs Eunice Tourell was the school secretary and also provided music to accompany the school singing. Caretaking, catering, and cleaning were also provided at a high standard.

It soon became apparent that the older pupils had suffered somewhat by the differing styles of teaching of recent years and needed a readjustment period. They responded readily to a 'middle of the road' approach and together we settled into an easy relationship mode. Like nearly all country children they made friends easily, responded to discipline and were a joy to teach.

The rabbits caused some concern at times but also provided amusement... 'May I borrow the school buck this weekend please?' or gems like... 'I cannot understand how that happened! I only put them together while I cleaned out the hutches!!' Good homes were found for all of them, you'll be glad to hear!

Our Educational Visits were mainly limited to one annual journey, sometimes to the seaside for a 'Fun Day'. We had an arrangement with the local coach company that we would decide our destination according to the weather. Secretly I think that many prayers were said for fine weather and a journey to the coast. I never really discovered why it was always the same child who became 'lost'.

Sporting activities figured quite frequently in our lives....Physical Education, Gymnastics, Football, Netball, Rounders, and Cricket; all had a place in the scheme of things, as did a Summer Sports Day and mildly competitive matches against other schools. I recall that we had some very able performers and that our Netball team performed with remarkable skill. I wonder if the High Jump record set by Leslie Terry was ever equalled or beaten?"

Mrs Betty Roberts, Mr Bill Lailey and Miss Audrey Amabilino in 1960

Mr and Mrs Lailey photographed in April 2002

Miss Amabilino with her Infant class of 1959

Mr Lailey with his Junior class of 1959

116

Miss Amabilino with her Infant class of 1960

The Junior class of 1960

Mr Lailey and his Upper Junior class of 1960

A rather 'leaning' group of 1961

Mr Lailey may have had happy memories of Froyle School but so did many of those who were taught by him. Roger Hayman-Start (1954 -1960) penned this ditty to commemorate his time at school.

OH HAPPY (SCHOOL) DAYS!

Of your planned publication re. Froyle School I have read
So here are some thoughts off the top of my head,
Of my time at Froyle School when I was a nipper
With Mrs Dean then Bill Lailey, known as the 'Skipper'

With Miss Amabilino, whom everyone fancied
And small bottles of milk which often went rancid,
Of getting the cane one dark winter's morn
For lobbing said bottles onto next door's front lawn~

Of when Mr Lailey put the football team up
For the match against Binsted, would we win the cup?
Up to the College where we played on a slope
Never much skill but we always had hope.

Of the time when the flasher jumped out on a lass
As we ran through the Beeches shouting en masse
How the police were called in but the flasher not found
No one could describe him, he just went to ground.

Of learning our tables, two five's are ten
Saying them over and over again,
And the same with our spelling, a twice weekly test
Would we remember, who would do best?

Of the day that I sang along with the choir
Despite being tone deaf, my voice was quite dire!
So I mimed with the others, passed Mari Hester a letter
Then had to say sorry, I should have known better.

Of learning for three years until I was ten
The history of Froyle Church again and again,
School plays at Christmas, paper chains and balloons,
Sports Days in summer with eggs and with spoons.

Each summer was sunny, each winter much snow.
Horseplay and laughter, little sadness or woe,
Marbles and conkers, kiss chase and tag,
Gobstoppers, sherbet dips and the odd lucky bag.

I look at old photos, the names I still know
How are they doing, where did they go?
The years have gone by but we all can recall
Our own happy thoughts of our own village school.

Although the 11+ exam had gone, there was still selection at 11 for 'grammar' or 'modern' secondary schools aided by an Intelligence Test and assessment by the pupils primary schools. Parents could choose whether they wished their child to take the selection tests. Selection procedures varied and there were meetings of area headteachers to discuss the best means of selection, standard English and Arithmetic tests being recommended at one point. The C.E.O. was invited to many P.T.A. meetings to talk on 'Secondary Education in the Country'. A few Froyle children were selected for a grammar education at Eggars but the majority transferred to the Alton Secondary Modern School. Doubtful children were referred to as 'border zone' and there was additional discussion before deciding which children should be invited to fill the remaining available grammar school places. Parents, of course, were allowed no access to school records, but relied on a termly school report of their child's progress - some schools still marked out of 10 or 100, others schools gave grades instead; A+ to E-!! There was space for comments on the county report forms and teachers sometimes assessed both ability and effort by grades.

The school accounts were regularly audited and there was now a suggestion that the school might open a 'Direct Spending' Account in addition to the ordinary school banking account. Finance in the past had all been dealt with through the County and stock obtained through the County's Central Purchasing scheme, or approved suppliers. At this time there was a separate allowance for books only. The P.T.A. began raising funds for 'little extras' for the school but generally all the main school needs were still supplied by the County.

School Outing to Bognor in 1962

120

Out of school visits continued to Chessington and Regent's Park Zoos. The older children were taken to the film 'The Ten Commandments' and a performance by the Children's Theatre in Alton. Annual outings were still to Bognor or Hayling Island. There was still a close connection with the Church, first with Reverend Field and, after 1961, with Reverend Walley; services for Harvest, Christmas, Lent and Easter usually being held in the Church. Each year an 'Easter Garden' was made by the children for the Church - a tradition which carried on until the closure of the school.

Ask any youngster who was at school during Mr Lailey's Headship and they will always come up with two particularly special memories. The first is of the Christmas Concert and Pantomimes put on every year and the second, Open Day! At first these Concerts used temporary staging, but when this was borrowed and disappeared Mr R.James, Drama Adviser, arranged for separate stage blocks and steps to be delivered. Curtains were erected across the room for the stage. Andrew Pritchard (1961-1967) remembers them well and one in particular!

"Mr Lailey used to produce some marvellous Christmas Pantomimes, all in rhyme. I remember us doing 'Sleeping Beauty'. Mark Elston, Barry Cousins and myself were three pantomime fairies, complete with frilly skirts and knickers.

I still remember our opening lines:-

> We're Pantomime Fairies, our duty is clear,
> We stand here before you, year after year.
> In order that we can announce in rhyme,
> The story each year of our own pantomime.
> This year has presented a problem or two,
> Because we couldn't at first decide what to do.
> Snow White or Cinderella, or the story of Dick,
> That lucky young fellow who became Mayor of London,
> A long time ago!
> After a great deal of fuss,
> We decided Sleeping Beauty suited us.
> Although we're short of beauty, you'll agree,
> We're probably the sleepiest lot you'll ever see."

It would seem that it became a tradition for three boys who would be leaving the following year to don the skirts, wigs and wands! Interestingly, we came across a report of Andrew's Panto in the local newspaper, the Alton Herald. Perhaps this will bring back a few memories to some of you!

"Froyle School Entertainment.

The children of Froyle School presented their annual concert for parents and friends on Friday. Both the afternoon and evening performances were given to a 'full house' of keen supporters. The younger members of the school presented a play, written by their class teacher, Mrs B.Roberts, in which a large number of delightfully costumed nursery rhyme characters invaded the dream world of a small girl, played by Caroline Elston, who dreamed that she was taken by Mother Goose (Jane Andrew) on a journey into Nursery-rhyme Land, where she met the Queen of Hearts (Sally Cousins), the Knave (Martin Wimshurst), Miss Muffet (Susan Hammett), Little Boy Blue (David Blunt), Simple Simon (Bobby Mustchin), the Pieman (Silvio Mirando), Bo Peep (Carol Alder), Jack & Jill (Ian Gunning & Joan Douglas) and a full supporting cast of Children who lived in a Shoe, their mother being played by Patricia Ottley. The part of Old King Cole was portrayed by Edwin Fry, complete with his Page and Fiddler (Stephen Blunt and Gareth Webb). The stage management duties were ably carried out by David Framp and Carol Watkins played the part of the little girl's mother.

This play was followed by the Pantomime, 'Sleeping Beauty', spoken in verse which was a blend of modern colloquialisms and old English. This pantomime was enthusiastically performed by the junior section of the school. The parts of the 'good' Fairies were hilariously played by three boys, Andrew Pritchard, Barry

Cousins and Mark Elston. They were suitably gowned and wigged in traditional manner and even managed a fairy dance. The King and Queen (Gary Kent & Susan Webb) gave a convincing performance as the proud parents of the Princess Clarabelle (Irene Woodcock), Laura Olivieri made an excellent nurse, Patricia Knight, as the wicked Fairy, gave an exceptionally good performance as did Paul Cousins as the Court Herald. The hero Prince (Peter Mustchin) and his Page (Janet Webb) roused the Princess from her sleep, assisted by the Woodcutter (Stephen Benniman)."

Unfortunately, or perhaps fortunately, as far as Andrew is concerned, we do not have a photograph of him as a fairy, but the one above is from the same Pantomime when it was performed in 1961.

At 'Open Day' each year the children's work was on view with dancing and P.E. displays, also Infant percussion work and often a Bring and Buy Sale was organised for school funds. Once more the Herald reporter was on hand to capture the special moments. To illustrate this article from the Herald we have included a series of photographs of Open Days, some taken by Mr Lailey, others by his wife. Although they do not relate to the specific year reported, they do give us an idea of what went on.

"School Open Day.

Froyle Primary School Open Day went with a swing on Thursday afternoon of last week. Although there was a smaller gathering of parents and friends than in the past, this was not due to lack of enthusiasm but to the fact that the number of children now attending the school is rather less than in previous years. Following what has now become their usual custom, the older girls had made delightful buttonholes for all their visitors and teachers.

Flower Sellers, July 1960

Raffle (below), July 1961

The boys had arranged shooting, bowling and fortune telling games in aid of school funds and there were also bring and buy and jumble stalls. Mrs Fry won the bowling game and also a box of chocolates in the Draw. A large basket of fruit was awarded to Mrs Eve from the other Draw.......

......While the children were active with the games and stalls, Mr W.Lailey, the Headmaster, and Mrs Roberts, who teaches Infants and the younger Juniors, were able to talk to parents who enquire about the progress of their offspring.

The second half of a very happy afternoon was spent watching the children engage in some of their more lighthearted school activities. The Infants recited poems to a most appreciative audience and demonstrated very colourful hand puppets they had made. Then the Juniors performed some charming country dances and gave a physical training display.

The Headmaster thanked all the parents for their continued support in school activities and expressed the wish that he would see them again at the sports day next week."

Many improvements were made to the school kitchen in this decade during which there were complete changes of kitchen staff. The gas cooker, pronounced out of date by the meals organiser, was overhauled, also the refrigerator. Wall heating was installed and the clock repaired.

There were a few more serious accidents. One girl fell out of the sweet chestnut tree during a P.E. lesson, fracturing her wrist and dislocating her elbow. One little boy died from leukaemia after a long illness. The Headteacher attended the child's funeral with Mrs Roberts, the boy's teacher and they also represented the school at the funeral of the late headmaster, Mr Knight, at the end of 1961.

There were some closures, notably for the wedding of Princess Margaret and the 750th Anniversary of Magna Carta, but also for local and general elections and when teachers went on an area training course.

The Cycling Proficiency Scheme came into operation, instruction being given by local policemen and the Headmaster. School football, netball, rounders and cricket teams played against several other local schools and the girls were generally more successful than the boys, but they all enjoyed the games and the company of other schoolchildren.

The Netball Team photographed in March 1961

Bill Lailey had only really just got himself settled into a "very pleasant and happy 'family' routine", when, in 1962, that routine was suddenly disturbed by the Education Department suggesting that it might be necessary to close the school down.

> *"A meeting was held in the school to discuss the possibility of a new school. It was unanimously agreed that a new school was desirable and the County were urged to proceed as quickly as possible. The Managers proposed that, should this be a long term project, then waterborne sanitation should be provided to serve the existing buildings. The question of siting was discussed, & in view of the fact that the population of the school was mainly centred in Lower Froyle, it was agreed that that would be the most likely and convenient place to build."* (November 1962)

We were fortunate to come by a report of that actual meeting, written by the correspondent to the school managers, Mr Tourell and we quote it in full, overleaf.

"Report on meeting held at Froyle School on Thursday, 8th November, 1962, at 4.15pm.

Present:

Froyle School Managing Body:
F.W.Heywood, Esq., M.A. (Chairman)
Mrs P.Bush
Mrs M.Milne
Mrs K.Newton-Davis
Lt.Col.C.Newton-Davis, M.C.
Rev.R.Whalley

County Council Representatives
A.J.Hardcastle, Esq., (Asst County Architect)
J.M.Swindlehurst, Esq., (Assistant Education Officer for Buildings)

In attendance:
Headmaster of Froyle School
Correspondent to Froyle School Managers.

The Chairman of the School Managers, after introducing the County representatives to the Managers, opened the meeting by explaining that the sanitation system at the school had for a very long time been a matter of primary concern to the School Managers themselves and to the parents of the pupils at the school. It would continue to be a primary concern if the suggestion of building a new school in Froyle meant a long delay. The Chairman referred the representatives to the County Education Officer's letter of 4th April, 1962, wherein the Managers had been informed that the County Architect was, in fact, proceeding with the conversion of the existing sanitary offices to a waterborne system.

Mr Swindlehurst explained that the Authority had now considered that the adaptation or conversion of the school generally was not an economic proposition and that the problem of maintenance over a number of years might involve a financial burden running very closely to the total capital expenditure of a new school. As a minor project (within the expenditure of £20,000) no special sanitation would be needed, and the question of priority would not arise. Provided there were no difficulties as to the site of a new school, he visualised the completion of a new building some time in 1963 or, allowing for minor delays, certainly by 1964. It was pointed out to the managers that the District Valuer would co-operate fully in the acquisition of a suitable site, and it was not anticipated at present that negotiations need be protracted once the planning and valuation departments had been informed of the chosen site for the new school.

The cost of demolition of the present building need not necessarily be considered as a large part of the minor project cost, since some demolition contractors engaged by the Authority were able to find a market for salvaged materials and thus carry out demolition work at a nominal figure.

The Managers and County representatives considered at some length the advantages and disadvantages of rebuilding the school on its present site, and it was mentioned by the Headmaster that, of the 49 children now attending the school, 41 lived in Lower Froyle. It was thought that the parents might prefer the school to be situated in Lower Froyle, yet there had been no evidence that the distance from pupils' homes to school had in any way contributed to unusual absences in the winter months. The representatives saw no objection to the location of a new school in Lower Froyle, but suggested that the site chosen should be well within the village boundary to avoid any overlapping of the catchment area of a neighbouring school.

Mr Hardcastle explained that a new school would accommodate 60 pupils, and be capable of an additional classroom should circumstances make necessary a larger intake.

Mr Hardcastle, in confirmation of a point mentioned by his colleague, explained to the Managers that a conversion of the present sanitation to a modern system would involve an expenditure far beyond the Managers' assessment. All fitting and units involved in the conversion would have to conform to the Ministry of Health standards, and, in the event that a main drainage scheme be provided for the village in the comparatively near future, the materials used in the conversion would largely prove unusable on a link-up of the school to the main district plant.

The general agreement of the managers and representatives was that a modern school, to be provided in 1963/1964, would prove to be the best solution, and that its location in Lower Froyle would be the wiser plan if it were to be built so as to serve the centre of population. In view of the building development that had taken place in that part of the village in recent years, a modern school building would not be out of place as might otherwise be the case if Upper Froyle were chosen for the new school premises.

An area of 1¾ acres being needed for a school, the managers were promised that a large-scale map would be made available for their indication and recommendation of suitable sites, and it was confirmed by the representatives that the Authority would take all necessary action for acquisition and planning.

The Headmaster, through the Managers, asked the representatives if he might make known to parents the possibility of the building of a new school when the next general meeting of the Parent-Teacher Association was held. He explained that parents were constantly asking as to the progress of the modern sanitation scheme, and the anticipation of new school premises would be an encouragement to them. The representatives had no objection to this disclosure, provided no attempt were made to anticipate the location of the new school premises before the Authority had confirmed the position with the School Managers.

The meeting closed at 5.30pm. The Chairman thanked the County officials for their attendance at the meeting, and for the help and advice offered to the managers. Reciprocal thanks were tendered.

(signed) L.J.Tourell, Correspondent to Froyle School Managers."

The next month, as promised, a large scale map was provided for the Managers.

"A meeting of the Managers was held to mark the map, provided by the County, with possible sites for the proposed new school. The most popular choice decided upon was opposite the Westburn Fields housing estate, on land farmed by Mr Thomas and owned by Mrs Bootle-Wilbraham."   *(December 1962)*

And then everything went quiet and as Mr Lailey had heard nothing for a couple of months, he rang Mr Swindlehurst,

"Rang Mr.Swindlehurst in order to discover if any progress had been made towards the provision of a new school for Froyle...."

The answer he got was not the one he wanted to hear!

"He stated that they were considering the possibility of an amalgamation with Bentley School."   *(March 1963)*

This news must have come as a bombshell to staff and parents. The idea of a brand new school would have been most appealing to all concerned, but then, suddenly, the idea of amalgamation with Bentley was quite another matter.

But the attendance figures were against them. Numbers had already begun to fall and in September 1963 the school had to revert to two teachers.

"School re-opened this morning. Three new pupils admitted, total number 43. School now re-organised as a two teacher school, Mrs B.Roberts in charge of infant and lower juniors, headmaster in charge of 2nd, 3rd and 4th year juniors."

Miss Amabilino had taught the Infant Class until she resigned at Easter 1961, but she returned, now as Mrs Hill, as a supply teacher for several years. Mrs Tourell, whilst officially school secretary, helped out in the school kitchen in cases of illness and also helped occasionally in the Infant Class or on school outings.

In January 1964 came the news everyone was dreading. The log book entry reads,

"It was confirmed that the closure of Froyle School would take place at some unspecified date in the future and the children of Froyle would be transported to a new school to be built at Bentley."

Bill Lailey remembers it well, "Naturally the staff were alarmed and we started to look for teaching posts in a more secure situation. It was at this time that I successfully applied for a Headship of a Primary School at Hordle on the edge of the New Forest. A larger school than Froyle but with the same friendly supportive parents offering assistance and friendship identical to that enjoyed during my years at Froyle."

As it happened Mr Lailey and his staff would have been quite secure in their positions at Froyle. The amalgamation with Bentley School did take place, but not until 1986!

Leslie Terry concentrating hard on his knitting

Indeed, back in 1964, after all the uncertainty and as the plans would only be executed at a future date, great effort was made to improve the present premises. The end of the Junior classroom nearest the corridor was finally partitioned off as a staff and children's cloakroom. There were now less than 50 children in school, so large classrooms were no longer a necessity. The suggested indoor toilet for the staff cloakroom never materialised - 'levels were too difficult' being the reason given! Handbasins and drinking fountains were eventually provided in both Infant and Junior cloakrooms. Roof repairs, floor renovation and both interior and exterior decorating were discussed and the buildings were all improved during this time. As we have seen above, for many years flush lavatories had been promised but delayed for various reasons, such as shortage of money, the laying of a completely new water mains for the village or schemes involving the collaboration of Treloar College and its sanitary arrangements. The College, in its infancy, had many plans for renovating and extending premises, involving the assistance of the Rural District Council. It was hoped that their sanitary scheme would enable Froyle School to follow suit, but the plans were abandoned due to lack of money.

The College, an Independent one, was catering for handicapped children suffering from TB or Polio and aimed to train the 'crippled' children for suitable practical skills so that they could earn a living. These skills included shoemaking, gardening, tailoring and, later, wireless and electronic skills and they were happy to co-operate with Froyle School at times. The College field was used for games until Mrs Bootle-Wilbraham offered the loan of the field opposite the school for Sports Days. This field would still be owned by her, but would be serviced by the County groundsmen.

School Sports Day July 1964

Parents, Managers, advisers and H.M.I.s persisted with requests for better sanitation. Mr Lailey's entry in the log book of March, 1961, gives a hint of how frustrating the whole episode was proving for the School,

> *"Parent-teacher meeting to discuss School Sanitation. Letter of protest signed by parents & staff sent to R.D.C."*

This letter appears to have had little effect on the 'powers that be', as it isn't until September 1963 we find another mention of sanitation work,

> *"Letter from C.E.O. stating that sanitation and toilet work would probably be carried out during term time. No indication as to which term!"*

Finally, in the Spring of 1964, after many delays, Milwards, the local Alton builders, commenced on the work of installing flush lavatories. The pupils were obliged to use portable Elsan closets in the Schoolhouse outbuildings, while water was laid on from the road and the buildings were adapted. Wash basins were not provided in the children's toilets as in the staff toilet, so the children still had to walk back into school to wash their hands, often forgetting to do this after the interval! There were still no wash basins in the toilets at the close of the school in 1986! Mr Lailey must have been delighted to finally write in the log book in May, 1964,

> *"Rang Winchester - toilet block is complete and buckets no longer require emptying."*

The toilets, when completed, were rather dark and cold in winter, so work was finally permitted to start on an electricity supply to the toilet block, for lights and for wall heaters. Heating in school was not very satisfactory either, the stoves smoked, jackdaws nested in the chimneys - this was prevented by putting wire nets at the tops of the chimneys, but they became clogged and the chimneys smoked again. Eventually, in the summer of 1964, central heating was to be installed with a new boiler during the holidays. The boiler arrived in September and, after installation, was lit in October, the caretaker, Mrs Terry, having been instructed by the engineer on stoking it! The engineer did warn that there might be trouble with draughts and the boiler did not function properly for some time; the radiators would not heat because of faulty valves and the system did not really work well until a small, electric, booster pump was installed at the end of the year. Then, although it now worked well, most of the heat went up into the roof space so 'drop ceilings' were fitted, also fluorescent lighting at the same time. Even then it was a case of trial and error to find the best fuel for the boiler. This stove presumably lasted for 20 years until superseded by an efficient gas fired heater. Various caretakers battled with the huge Robin Hood stove and its long rakes. It took up a large amount of space - halfway along the middle classroom floor! It always seemed temperamental, burning well on warmer days and going out on really cold ones! The school secretary often had to deal with it in the daytime. As the large-bore central heating pipes went round the classrooms just above floor level, all the cupboards had to be raised on plinths so that they could fit back against the walls.

Externally, the front boundary wall of the school was causing problems where tree roots had undermined it, and it was in a state of near collapse. After much discussion and the visiting of the school by various County officials, it was decided to demolish part of the wall and to provide vehicular access to the school premises at the Vicarage side of the school. This would make delivery of stock and fuel etc. much easier and would enable the school dental caravan to be parked on the premises with a nearby water supply. The wall had to be restored to match the other walls in the village. Many of the Upper Froyle stone walls had been built by Napoleonic prisoners of war from local 'malmstone' and this stone was used for both the school and the schoolhouse. A metal tubular double gate was erected and this caused much environmental criticism, for although the site was not yet a conservation area, the attractive appearance of the village as a whole was carefully guarded! The gate was not replaced, but as a concession it was painted a dark green!

In July 1965 Mr Lailey spoke to Mrs Bootle-Wilbraham regarding the Sports field.

"I had an interview with Mrs Bootle-Wilbraham to discover if it is possible to obtain the use of the paddock, used for Sports Day, as the school Playing Field. She appeared most anxious to co-operate in this matter, and if all goes well with Mr Andrew, her tenant farmer, the School Managers and the County Education Authority, the school should eventually have a playing field of its own."

All obviously did go well with Mr Andrew, as in January 1966 Mr Lailey writes,

"Met Mr W.Andrew, tenant farmer of the piece of land proposed for playing field area, discussed with him the fencing off of the area."

And finally, in April that year,

"County Playing Fields staff today erected a gate into the playing field area loaned by Mrs Bootle-Wilbraham."

Also in 1966 the flagstone floors of the entrance hall, corridor and both cloakrooms were replaced by thermoplastic tiling. At this time all unnecessary chimneys were demolished and clear glass, reinforced against footballs and marbles, put into the previously diamond-leaded window panes in most of the school windows, but the managers objected to the demolition of the school bell-tower unless it was unsafe. They felt that it would detract from the attractive appearance of the school, which was likened to a church building by many, over the generations.

Thus a substantial overhaul of the school buildings was completed by the time Mr Lailey resigned his post at the end of the Summer Term, 1966, to take up his headship in Hordle. Mrs Roberts agreed to be Acting Headteacher for one term until another appointment could be made.

Methods in the teaching of Mathematics were changing and the Infant Adviser, Miss Bradburn, came into school to instruct staff and children in the use of 'Cuisinaire' rods (coloured wooden rods of graduated lengths). Standard measure was still in use, until the Seventies. School equipment was improving and new locker desks were provided. The school acquired a radio and speaker (standard county supply) also a typewriter and, later, a cassette player.

Farewells to Mr Lailey were made at the summer 'Open Day' where he was presented with a wrist watch, a pair of secateurs and a bottle of wine! He thanked the staff, parents and managers for their co-operation and said that he had enjoyed the friendly atmosphere at the school. There was a farewell end of term service in the Church, taken by Reverend Cummings, and Mr Lailey returned to school during the holidays, to complete the hand-over procedure. He is remembered to this day, as being an excellent Headmaster and teacher and a very special person.

At the beginning of Mrs Roberts' term as Headteacher, Mrs Simpson came in to teach the Infant Class and the new Vicar, Reverend L. Pickett, arrived. The number on roll for this term was 41. The roof was retiled - a lengthy job - and the Marley flooring in the cloakrooms was completed. At the end of September, Mrs Moore joined the staff as a part time 'supernumerary' or ancillary helper. Older Juniors took part in a performance of 'Noyes Fludde' at the Alton Secondary School, a joint primary/secondary district effort. Cycling proficiency badges and certificates were presented by an Rural District Councillor, Mrs Thomson-Glover, at a P.T.A. meeting, with a talk by Sgt Warrell of Alton on 'Road Safety' with slides and films on the subject.

The office radiator leaked and was repaired and there was talk of interior decoration in the near future. Windows were repaired at the rear of the school. Several football and netball matches were played and in November, Miss Freda Swain, who had been appointed the new Headteacher for January 1967, visited the school. Staff attended a lecture at the new Mathematics Centre at the Winchester Teachers Centre. There were two performances of the school Christmas Concert and presentations made to Mrs Roberts and Mrs Tourell who were leaving the school. A Christmas party and a Christmas service in Church, with children reading the lessons, ended the term successfully.

Mr Lailey's Photo Album

Christmas Party in 1960

Class 2 P.E. in the Autumn of 1961

All smiles in the Autumn of 1961

Playing with Dinky toys

Mothers meeting, Open Day 1961

A needlework class in June 1961

P.E. Lesson in October 1962

A snowball fight in the winter of 1963

Christmas Parties

Sporting teams of 1965

'Cockerell' Tapestry, completed in the Summer of 1966

A happy Sports Day group in 1966

The Waning Years

THE   NATIONAL   SOCIETY

PATRON: HER MAJESTY THE QUEEN

The Society desires to convey its congratulations to

Froyle Church of England School

on the occasion of the

1867 *Centenary* **1967**

of the foundation of this School of the Church of England,
and records with pride the witness which this School
has made to true education and the maintenance of the
Christian Faith in the tradition established through the ages
since the first Church School was founded in the Sixth Century

Given under the hands of His Grace the President, the Chairman, and
the General Secretary:

Archbishop of Canterbury

Chairman

General Secretary

141

The year 1967 was quite a memorable one for Froyle School. Not only did it have a new Headmistress, Miss Freda Swain, and a new teacher, Mrs Trinkwon, but it was also the centenary of its actual founding. At this time there were just 39 children on the roll. Mrs Kelly still came one day per week as 'peripatetic', but the Juniors had Miss Swain and the Infant Class Mrs Trinkwon as their new teachers. Mrs Wallinder acted as secretary for one week, after which her duties were taken over by Mrs B.Loughborough, until later in the year when she in turn was replaced by Mrs Fox.

There were many visitors to the school in those first few weeks; Mrs Barnard, the School Meals Organiser; Mr Chalmers, the Education Welfare Officer, and Mrs McKenzie, the Health Visitor. Later in the term visits by the Diocesan Director of Education, Miss Mitchell, H.M.I., and Miss Richards, the P.E. Organiser, were made. School life settled down to a routine that year, most of the major building improvements having been made previously; there were termly managers meetings, P.T.A. meetings, medical and dental visits and inspections, and regular visits from the Educational Medical Officer and school nurse. Sports were not forgotten, football and netball were played against neighbouring schools, there was joint swimming with Bentley School, with Sports and Inter-School Sports Days in the summer. Visits were made to Longleat and to the New Forest and the term ended with an Open Day, as reported in the Alton Herald below, and a visit from the H.M.I. for a General Inspection.

"Wednesday last week was another exciting day for the children of Froyle Church of England Primary School, for on that day parents and friends were invited to an open day to see the work they had done in the term. For the entertainment the juniors had made their own sideshows and had various raffles. Mrs Russell and Mrs Bellis kindly organised cups of tea in the afternoon, when all assembled to see the raffles drawn and the various prizewinners collect their prizes. One member of the school, Irene Woodcock, could not partake of the fun as she was in the Treloar Hospital, Alton, following an operation. Miss F.M.Swain, the headmistress, thanked everyone for coming along. The school closed on Friday for the summer holidays and the five children who were leaving received a book token."

When the Autumn term started in September 1967, a new teacher, Miss Frost, took over the Infant Class, there being 36 on roll. A service of thanksgiving was held in St Mary's Church on Sunday 10th September to mark the Centenary of the founding of Froyle School. One imagines that celebrations were also held in school, or were they perhaps held the following year in celebration of the actual opening of the building rather than its founding? We simply do not know. Unfortunately for the historian, Miss Swain was a writer of very few words and her entries in the log book make no mention whatsoever of any special celebrations during either 1967 or 1968. We do have a photograph, however.

Amongst those depicted above are:

Back row, left to right
- , Sally Cousins, Linda Stemp, Deborah Everard?, Pat Ottley, - , Linda Ottley, Carol Watkins, Caroline Elston, Teresa Watkins, Joan Douglas.

Middle row, left to right
Andrew Terry, Edwin Fry, Rennie Green, Jonathan Adams, - , Sarah Morris.

Front row, left to right
Martin Pritchard, Richard Westwood, Mark Elston, Ian Gunning, Beverley Fry, Silvio Mirando, Barry Cousins, David Framp.

Miss Swain, who had come to Froyle from the New Forest, could perhaps have been a little more tactful when stating, only a few months after taking up her headship, that she had "...taught gypsies (in her last school) and they were far better behaved than Froyle children." This did not go down at all well with many of the parents, who had enjoyed an excellent relationship with the previous Head.

By January 1968 the roll had fallen to 34 and Miss Swain met parents who were concerned about the future of the school. There was, however, no further mention of school closure or amalgamation during the rest of the decade. The 11 + selection procedure took place each year, one or two children being offered 'grammar school' places or considered 'border zone' cases. When Miss Swain was absent with illness for a few days in March 1968, the school was run by Mr B.Head, deputy head of Alton C.E. School. Mrs Shipley took up duty as school secretary in April 1968 and, as in most years then, there were students from King Alfred's College in Winchester on observation or teaching practice. Miss Coulson, Diocesan R.E. Adviser, visited the school in May and at the end of the summer term the Juniors visited Carisbrooke Castle and Osborne House on the Isle of Wight, followed by an Open Day with displays of work done.

In September 1968, Miss P.J. Rache took over the Infant Class, Miss Frost having resigned at the end of the summer term. Teachers now annually attended a 'Refresher Course' at Winchester, they went on a French course at Fareham and the Headteacher attended the annual Headteachers' Conference in Basingstoke. Seasonal services were attended in Church and the Vicar came into school to teach both Infants and Juniors each week. In October 1968 Miss Swain was called for jury service and the school was in the charge of Mrs Kelly, or Mrs Meager on her days of absence from school.

In 1969 the school gas meter was adapted. Mr J.Killick, the Primary Adviser, and Mr P.Laver, Assistant Primary Adviser, visited the school during the spring term. Children visited the New Forest and took part in the Alton Music Festival and Inter-School Sports took place at Binsted. Miss Roche resigned at the end of the summer term and in September Mrs Sharron Enticknap took over her duties. There were still 36 children on roll, made up of 13 Infants and 23 Juniors. Sharron Enticknap taught the Infant class and remembers that, of the thirteen children, five were left-handed. Fortunately Sharron's husband was also left-handed so this helped in her bid to ensure that their education didn't suffer. She also remembers school dinners and one little girl in particular who had auburn hair - was that you? - and hated salad on Fridays. "She used to cry every Friday because she didn't want to eat that 'green stuff with legs' - mustard and cress!!"

There were autumn visits to the Royal Wilton Carpet Factory near Salisbury and also to Old Sarum and Stonehenge. Head-lice were a problem during the term, two children being excluded by the school nurse. As well as the usual school Christmas entertainment, the children entertained some old people at a party in school. Teachers were invited to attend an exhibition of school furniture at Chandlers Ford; great changes were taking place in school equipment and apparatus. Children's books were changing, they were more attractive with better illustrations and some books were being replaced by 'teaching packs', programmed learning schemes and 'work-cards'. The staff visited the progressive Reading Centre at Reading University, run by Mrs Betty Root, to look at new reading books and schemes.

Outings in 1970 and 1971 were to the New Forest and to Windsor Safari Park. Visits to the school by the peripatetic remedial teacher, Mr Thompson, began to help individual children with their special needs, also often supplying specialist books and equipment. These visits by him continued for some years. At the annual Open Day in the summer there was a sale of work for school funds.

In September 1971 Miss Lesley Harrison took over the Infant Class as Mrs Enticknap was leaving the school in November. Mrs Shipley took on ancillary duties in addition to her secretarial work and Mrs Goodyear commenced duties as kitchen helper. Miss Wyman, the Infant Adviser, visited the school and there were children's visits to the Brighton Aquarium, Fishbourne Roman Palace and Cowdray House.

In January 1972 there were 38 children on roll. Following dental inspection and treatment, a dental film was shown to the children. In May there was an Inter-School Quiz with Binsted School, which was won by Froyle! Outings took place to Singleton, Chichester Harbour, Birdworld and Abbotstone; the term ended with Inter-School Sports, this time at Bentley, and an Open Day. Mrs Kelly left at the end of the term, to be replaced by Mrs BettyRoberts in a reorganisation of the peripatetic teachers areas.

During the year 1972/73 numbers on roll rose from 37 to 47. There were two concentrated swimming courses of three weeks during the year, at Odiham R.A.F. pool. The P.T.A. organised a 'Bingo' evening in the autumn and the A.G.M. was held in the summer with an Open Evening. The teachers attended a publishers exhibition in Winchester and the younger children visited a newsagents and confectioners shop in Alton; the Juniors visiting Danebury hill fort.

In March 1973, with numbers rising, Miss Swain had written to the County Education Officer asking for a part-time teacher. As the Autumn term got under way with no less than 51 children on roll, Mrs Sonia Hall joined the staff. She was in school mostly in the mornings to work with groups of children in basic subjects. Mrs L.Lyne joined the staff as an ancillary helper for two hours daily. There was a day's holiday for the wedding of Princess Anne. At Christmas an entertainment was held as usual and there was a party given by the P.T.A. in the Village Hall.

At a P.T.A. meeting in January 1974, Mrs Cook, the Health Education Officer, gave a slide and film show on 'Sex Education in Schools'. In February Mrs Terry resigned her position as caretaker and was replaced by Mr Kelly from the College. By April there were 56 on roll, the highest number for some years. There was another swimming course at Odiham. The two students at the school in the summer term joined in outings to the New Forest and to the Kennet and Avon Canal, with a cruise on the horse drawn barge to Hamstead Lock! In April the same year, the school Morris team, trained by Miss Ireson, from the English Folk Dance Society, gave a demonstration of Morris Dancing at the Butts School in Alton. Mr James (A.E.O.) visited the school in July. The term closed with the customary A.G.M. of the P.T.A. and an Open Evening.

The autumn term of 1974 was to be the last term for Miss Swain at the school, before retiring. A new Headteacher, Mrs Nora Jupe, from Basingstoke, had been appointed during the summer holidays and was to take up duty in January 1975. Numbers had dropped to 46 on roll, when Mr Victor Lark joined the school as peripatetic Headteacher relief. Mrs Lynes was replaced by Mrs O.Weaden as ancillary helper in mid-September. A King Alfred's College student, Mr McAlpine, spent October and November in the school on his final teaching practice. Mrs Jupe paid three visits to the school during the term to become acquainted. She also attended the end of term Christmas entertainment when a presentation of a coffee percolator, cream jug, sugar basin and cheque was made to Miss Swain on her retirement. Mr R.James, from Mid-Hampshire Education Office, presented her with a 'golden letter' from the Authority. Term ended with the customary children's party given by the P.T.A.

The children perform at Miss Swain's farewell in December1974

The Final Years

HAMPSHIRE COUNTY COUNCIL

FROYLE C.E. (CONTROLLED) PRIMARY SCHOOL —
PROPOSED CLOSURE

1. **Notice is hereby given,** in accordance with the provisions of Section
   12(1) of the Education Act 1980, that the Hampshire County Council,
   being the Local Education Authority, **intend to cease to maintain the
   Froyle C.E. (Controlled) Primary School** in the parish of Froyle within
   the East Hampshire District with effect from 31st August, 1986.

2. In order to achieve this intention it is proposed that:
   (a) Education will cease to be provided in the premises of the Froyle
       C.E. (Controlled) Primary School at the end of the Summer Term,
       1986.
   (b) Children in attendance at that time (and not transferring to
       Secondary Schools) will, subject to (c) below, transfer to Bentley
       C.E. (Controlled) Primary School.
   (c) Applications for admission to alternative schools will be
       considered, subject to the availability of places.

The notice that ended 118 years of education in Froyle

When, in January 1975, Mrs Jupe became the tenth Headteacher of Froyle School, there was little indication that she was also to be the last one! In the sixties there had been great concern regarding closure, or of change of use to an Infant or 'First' school, but hopes of a new school building at Froyle had been dashed when it was suggested that, if there was a new building, it would be at Bentley and the older Froyle children, at least, would attend it. However, as nothing had materialised, life went on at Froyle as normal.

The seventies brought many educational changes, both nationally and regionally. At the end of Mrs Jupe's first term the County administration reorganised into eight smaller areas, still with a County Education Officer at the helm, but with eight Area Officers in their own premises and with their own administrative staffs. Froyle benefited financially by the change as the County funded some improvements at the beginning of the year and later the area administration followed suit! This covered building and equipment and at this time money was usually available for suitable improvements, particularly when a school had a new headteacher. A new TV set, radio and tape recorder were quickly provided; roofs, gutters, playground surfaces, sinks and water heaters received attention and additional electric points were installed. Classrooms were rearranged and books added, also new bookcases, and a 'library corner' was arranged at the back of the Junior classroom, in place of a large guinea pig run, now obsolete, as the authorities no longer encouraged the keeping of animals in classrooms! Books were borrowed and exchanged from the County library mobile service, the number of books each term was now raised from 100 to 150.

Jane Waring (1973-79) remembers the library van, "The library van visited about once a month and we were allowed to take out one fiction and one non fiction book. This was always quite exciting because we had our own library cards and it was our choice as to what to choose. The funny thing is, how when you're a child you get things sort of muddled up, we also had the travelling dental van that used to come and camp in the playground probably once or twice a year and I always thought it was the library van in disguise! In fact I think it only came to mind years later that they were in fact two different vans!"

School based tests were given regularly to check progress. There were to be new County tests within a few years, with a new record system, but for the present, old record forms, orange for boys and green for girls, were filled in annually and school report forms, or books, and teachers 'Forecast and Record of Work' books were still available from the County, although not compulsory.

For two years the school continued with two classes and some part-time help; Mrs Jupe taking the Junior Class and Miss Lesley Harrison the Infant Class,

148

with Mrs Sonia Hall working half time taking groups of children from the Junior Class for special basic work and help. Wednesday continued to be the 'peripatetic' day for most of the remaining school years. Mr Victor Lark came into school for that one day each week, relieving the headteacher from her teaching duties to attend to the administrative work of the school. This also gave the Juniors extra help with music and handwork, Mr Lark's specialist subjects.

On the parent/teacher front the P.T.A. was enlarged to become 'Friends of Froyle School', in order to include outside members who were interested in the school. Regular meetings, invited outside speakers, and also social events were held, organised by an enthusiastic committee. Although this was welcomed by those of us who did not have children at the school and yet wished to be involved in activities there, it was not a particularly popular idea with parents and by 1980 a resolution to revert to a Parent/Teacher Association only had been put before the gathering at the Friends of Froyle School A.G.M. Those putting forward the proposals felt that the name 'Friends of Froyle' was misleading and could be misconstrued as having nothing to do with the school. Eventually a compromise was reached, so as not to exclude the 'Friends' and the association became 'Froyle School P.T.A. & Friends'.

There were many activities at the school during the year. Morris and Maypole dancing took place at a Festival in Alton and at the May Day celebrations. Miss P.Ireson, a member of the English Folk Dance Society, visited the school to teach the dances. A Knock-Out Competition between Bentley, Binsted, Holybourne and Froyle schools, preceded the School and Inter-School Sports Days.

Inter-School Sports 1975

A big change occurred for the 'school leavers' in 1975. For the first time the fourth year children moved on as one group to Eggars School in Alton, secondary education in Alton having been combined, with both Amery Hill and Eggars Schools becoming Comprehensive for the West and East areas of the town respectively. On their last day of term the Froyle leavers were given a paperback book, presented by Lt.Col.Willcocks, chairman of the governors.

1975 ended with a Friends of Froyle School 'Christmas in the Country' evening, a performance by the children of 'Christmas in Mexico' and a Nativity Service in the Church. On the last afternoon of term, a party, arranged by the parents, was held in the Village Hall.

The photograph above shows the children performing 'Christmas in Mexico' and this particular entertainment was Jane Waring's most memorable. She can be seen clasping her knees, seated in the second row, second from the right.

"We all dressed up in Mexican style costumes and sang songs from around the world. We made a pinyata which we all took turns to hit with a stick and break, inside it was full of sweets and lollies so there was an huge urgency to smash the thing to pieces. Mr Lark played the piano and we had a really big Christmas Tree in the hall. Father Christmas always came after the show and all the children got a present and then we had cakes and squash etc and something for the parents."

Jane shares some of her other memories of Froyle School with us,
"The P.E. shed was a treasure trove of very old (probably as old as the school)

equipment, porcelain eggs for the egg and spoon race, bean bags, cane hoops, coconut mats (oh, we hated having to sit on them - they made the top of your legs itch!), coloured bands to denote teams, loads of cricket equipment, stumps, bats & balls and the ribbons for the maypole. And the maypole - oh my, we hated this, it was so dangerous, boys had to sit on the middle crossovers to stop the thing crashing to the ground, which it did on several occasions.

One of the nice things about Froyle School was the toffee tin! If it was your birthday you were allowed to blow out the birthday candle and choose a toffee from the tin (mixed toffees from the village shop) I remember being so excited about it. I loved that tin! It was a really old Birds Toffee tin. The whole school was split into teams, Red, Blue, Yellow & Green. Family members stayed together in the teams and we has team points which we got through the week for being good or doing good work etc and these were noted in our team point books. At the end of the week they were totted up by the Team Leader and during the Friday assembly the winning team was announced and I think the whole team got a Toffee each from that lovely toffee tin!

The outside toilets were always dreaded by everyone, I was personally petrified by them. Not only were they very dark and dingy, in the winter they were so ice cold that the water would freeze over on the top of the toilet if it wasn't flushed often, some of the biggest spiders I have ever seen also lived in there. It was always a bit of a nightmare because there were no sinks in the toilet blocks you had to then run back to the school to wash your hands, Can you imagine this being allowed today!

We all took it in turns to ring the bell for playtime/lunch end of playtime etc. The hand bell was quite heavy and must have been really old and made a lovely sound it was one of those strange honours when it came round to your turn to ring it.

We were not allowed to use pens until the final year at Froyle, we were then issued with our own Beryl Blue pen and a Bic Biro, it was really exciting to be able to use pens after so long using pencils, but woe betide anyone who lost their pen or made a mess in their books with them because it would be back to pencils!"

Robert Brown, at school at the same time as Jane, remembers,

"The milk that came with its own permeating odour of feet, the out of tune piano, Mr Lark's gruff manner, his battered Peugeot, the Mini Estate of Mrs Jupe! and the ladies in the Office. The football matches against the playground wall, the dark alleys in the school, the sunbeams, the art on the walls. The playground had a wonderful view over fields and as beautiful as it was it also felt so isolating. The loos were a bit nasty; the classrooms musty, the sun shining through the tiny windows.

Mrs Jupe told me, 'When you reach thirty your burning ambition will

Miss Lesley Harrison with her Infant class of 1976

Mrs Nora Jupe with her Junior class of 1976 and Mr Victor Lark

make itself known and you'll find yourself.' - she was right!"

In the Spring term of 1976 Mrs Jupe was absent owing to illness and the death of her mother, and in the Summer Term was again absent for surgery at Basingstoke Hospital. During this time the school was run by Mr Burgess, Mr Lark and Mr P.Cockerham, respectively, before Mrs Jupe returned to duty on Monday, 19th July. By September there were staff changes; Mrs Hall moved to Bentley School for part time work, and Miss Harrison moved to a new post at Bordon School, so the Infant Class were taught by Mrs C.Taylor for a term.

In the Autumn the children made bread for the Harvest Service, and when an 'Australian Afternoon' was held in school, a surprising statistic emerged, no less than nine of the forty-nine children now at school had previously visited or lived in Australia! Christmas Festivities included a social Christmas evening, a performance of 'Cinderella' at the Lord Mayor Treloar College, a Nativity Service in Church, entitled 'Come Christmas', and the usual Christmas Dinner and Party.

1977 was a memorable one for the school. In January, Mrs Jones took over the Infant Class and a third class was formed, as numbers had now risen to 50. This was taken temporarily by Mrs S.Marsden and the school was promoted from Group I to Group II. Also in January 1977 Mrs Russell, who had been school cook for the past twelve years, had to resign as she was moving to Petersfield.

There was great excitement when a large bough fell off the Holm Oak tree in the playground in snowy weather, landing on Mrs Marsden's car, which fortunately only suffered a broken windscreen wiper!

The Alton Herald reported, "Children at Froyle Primary School were dismayed to find that a huge limb of a giant evergreen oak growing in their playground has collapsed on to their teacher's car during lessons on Thursday of last week. (13th January). They rushed to tell headmistress, Mrs N.Jupe, who found that the car, belonging to Mrs S.Marsden, was completely obscured by the heavy branch, which had cracked under the weight of the wet snow.

The branch was more than a foot thick, and only the fact that it remained partially attached to the trunk saved the car from being crushed. 'It was very lucky that no children were under the tree when it happened', said Mrs Jupe.

Mr W.Start, agent for the Froyle Estate Forestry team, was called in, and with a tractor and other gear, the men released the car, which was found to be undamaged except for a broken windscreen wiper.

The county grounds staff were called in to check the remainder of the tree, and pronounced it safe. The broken branch was sawn into logs and the adventure was over for the children - who this week provided a series of paintings and drawings depicting the incident. Several excellent efforts were offered to the Herald and our only way to select the one required, was to look for the work of the youngest artist. It happened that Stuart Pritchard had also managed, at 7½ years, a most striking (sorry, Miss!) piece of work."

At Easter Mrs Harris resigned as school caretaker and Mrs Rosemary Bennett took over the position, while Mrs Pat Woolford became the new school cook, both ladies being parents of children in the school.

On May 28th the school entered the third annual 'Knock-Out' Competition, held at Holybourne Andrews' Endowed School that year.

The Alton Herald covered the event,

"... The contest involved teams from Bentley, Binsted, Froyle and Holybourne Schools in games which ranged from the transporting of an 'Egyptian Mummy' to a pyramid, to rescuing a 'Damsel in Distress'. Excitement mounted as the games progressed and the scores became closer, until, at the end of the final game Froyle and Holybourne were equal with 26 points each, Binsted having 25 points and Bentley 19. The winners were decided by the 'Mini-Marathon', in which the teams had to paint squares to form the words 'Silver Jubilee'. Froyle, having completed more squares, were declared the winners by the referee, Mr B.Benham, Headmaster of Wootey Junior School. The other judges were members of Alton Lions. The shield was presented to Jackie Brambley, of Froyle's winning team, by the Rev. John Coutts, Vicar of Holybourne."

A very proud Mrs Jupe wrote in her log book on the following Monday,

"The children greeted the staff with the Shield which they had won at the Knock-Out Competition on Saturday. Mrs Jupe congratulated them all at Assembly and asked them to thank their parents for all the help given."

Froyle's winning team

On the following Thursday, June 2nd, the children experienced another memorable occasion, when they celebrated Her Majesty the Queen's Silver Jubilee. Plans had been made, some months beforehand, for a celebration to be held jointly at Treloar College and enough money was raised to buy each child a souvenir mug and specially minted 'Jubilee Crown' for the occasion. At 3.00 p.m. everyone went across to the Treloar College for a varied programme of songs, both patriotic and those popular during the past twenty-five years. These included 'Congratulations', 'Two Little Boys', 'Charlie is my Darling', 'Land of Hope and Glory' and, of course, 'God Save The Queen'. There were also Musical Drill, Recorder, Clarinet and Piano items. This musical entertainment was followed by a tea-party on the lawns, then a Punch and Judy show and balloon modelling, ending with an hour's display of country, morris and maypole dancing. Miss Ireson played guitar for Circassian Circle, Galopede, Bean Setting, Single Plait and Double Plait. She then presented the children with their Jubilee mugs and everyone went home, tired, but happy.

Some weeks earlier a Jubilee greetings card had been sent to the Queen. This was made by the older children with the help of Mrs Waring. A crest for the card was designed by a pupil, Brian Shurgold, with all the children signing the silver 'scraperboard' interior. A school photograph, taken especially to mark the occasion, was included with the card, showing the front of the school building with its red, white and blue decorations!

The picture that went to the Queen

The card, with a set of the specially printed Jubilee stamps, was posted at Alton Post Office by two fourth year girls, Sarah Woolford and Dawn Woodcock.

A letter from Buckingham Palace from the Queen's Lady-in-Waiting, thanking them for their card, was received some weeks later.

"To the Children and Staff of Froyle Primary School,

I am commanded by The Queen to write and thank you all for the good wishes which you sent Her Majesty on the occasion of her Silver Jubilee. The Queen was deeply touched that you should remember her at this time, and I am to tell you that your kind message has given Her Majesty great pleasure. I am to send to you all The Queen's most sincere thanks.

Susan Hussey, Lady in Waiting."

A nice touch to the letter was a hand written p.s. "The Queen thought your card had been beautifully made and decorated."

Celebrating the Silver Jubilee of Her Majesty the Queen in 1977

As a permanent memento of the Silver Jubilee, Mr & Mrs Hawthorne, parents of children in the school, gave a print of the Annigoni portrait of the Queen in her Garter robes. This was heat sealed and framed and hung in the school, reviving the tradition of earlier days, when schools always displayed a picture of the reigning monarch! Three trees and bushes, a blue ceanothus, a white spirea and a red hawthorn, were planted in the school grounds near the front gates.

In September 1977 Mrs Marsden was replaced by Miss A.Booker as a permanent teacher for the Middle Class, which had now settled well, using the hall as a classroom but, of course, having to clear it for school meals.

Jane Waring shares her favourite and not-so-favourite meals with us, "Spam fritters - I may be a vegetarian now but still dream of eating Spam Fritters! Spaghetti Bolognaise, but the spag was chopped up in to little pieces to stop messy slurping! Roast dinner, which was mostly chicken, served on Wednesdays only! Duchess potatoes. Pilchards with salad - aaahh, my most hated meal ever! Fish on Fridays; Sausages & Chips - well soggy slices of potato anyway! Macaroni Cheese, usually served with mixed veg, odd concoction I thought! Sweet & Sour pork with rice; Chicken & Veg pie with a crusty top; Freshly cooked bread rolls; Lemon Love Cake; Pineapple Upside Down Cake; Instant Whip; Gooseberry Crumble (yuck, yuck, yuck!)."

Having recovered from those memories, Jane goes on, "And another lunch time story was the water glasses. We had Pyrex tumblers that had a fill line near the top. We were only allowed to fill the glass to this line and I seem to remember Mrs Jupe being quite strict about this one glass each, mind you that may have had something to do with having outside toilets! On the bottom of each glass there was a number stamped into the glass. The first thing you did when you got your glass was look at the number and whoever had the highest number was the winner! When we had finished we had to scrape our plates into a metal bowl which went into the big pig bin outside which incidentally on a hot summers day smelt to high heaven as I think it was only collected once a week!"

Sadly, as 1977 drew to a close, the old Holm Oak was declared 'unsafe' by the County Arboricultural Officer, as honey-fungus had appeared at its base. A whole week was devoted to the felling of the tree, which had grown eight main trunks during its century of existence. This sadness was tinged with excitement, as the children watched and recorded the felling of the lordly old tree, making a 'tree box' for posterity. As the school was now within the 'Conservation Area' for Upper Froyle, a small Holm Oak tree was planted with

due ceremony near the old site. This new tree flourished until the sale of the premises in 1988, but when moved for the site of a new garage, it unfortunately died. Although the old tree no longer provided shade and shelter for the children it did however give them large trunks or logs to sit on or play on at break times in the playground.

At the beginning of 1978, Mrs Price resigned as non teaching assistant and Mrs Betty Waring took her place as afternoon ancillary helper for two hours each day. There were now 49 children on roll and, as there were many new parents, the staff decided to provide an 'Information Leaflet' for them. A copy of this has proved invaluable in researching the school's history, for even though we are only talking about things which were happening just 25 years ago, our memories tend to play tricks with us and become very selective!

So what do we learn from the leaflet? In 1978 the School Managers were Lt.Col.J.F.Willcocks (Chairman), Mr W.N.Greene (Vice Chairman), Mrs P.Morris, Mr D.Bennett, Mrs A.Andrew and Reverend K.Daubney. The Clerk to the Managers was Mr L.J.Tourell. The children were divided into three classes, Upper Junior, Lower Junior and Infants. These classes were taken by the Headteacher, Mrs Jupe, Miss A.Booker and Mrs J.Jones respectively.

There were two part-time ancillary helpers - Mrs K.Shipley assisting with secretarial work in the morning and Mrs Betty Waring with general help in the afternoon. In the kitchen Mrs Pat Woolford was cook, and she was assisted by a kitchen helper, Mrs Molly Goodyear and a Dining Room Assistant, Mrs N.Thorne. Mrs Rosemary Bennett was the caretaking cleaner-in-charge.

School uniform was not compulsory, but had been requested by some of the parents and, at a P.T.A. meeting, a parental majority voted that green should be the new school colour with red as an additional colour. Prior to this the school colours had been blue, but parents felt that if the uniform was green, items not outgrown could be worn on to secondary school, as Eggar's colour was also dark green. To distinguish it from other schools the tie would have a narrow red stripe and there would be blazer and cap badges with the letters 'FS' in red on a green background. The smaller badges were sewn on the girls green wraparound netball skirts, which they wore with white T-shirts and the boys wore green football shirts with white shorts. Grey, white and navy were all acceptable colours and, as we have said, it was not compulsory wear. Children's clothing in this decade was changing for more casual styles and, although primary schools could not dictate fashion, holiday type wear, fancy sandals and jeans were not encouraged.

Other details in the new leaflet included information on school organisation, curriculum, welfare services, school funds, etc. Parents were gradually being encouraged to take a greater interest in their children's schools and to help whenever possible. Gone were the days when schools displayed the notice, 'Parents not allowed beyond this door'!

Standards of football and netball were rising in the school, due both to the enthusiasm of the children and the coaching of Mr Bennett and Miss Booker with help from others, culminating in the girls winning a coveted trophy.

"The School took part in the Inter-Schools Rally which was held at Anstey School on Saturday, March 11th.

The boys Six-a-Side Football team reached the quarter-final stage. The team was:- A.Bennett, M.Waring, B.Shurgold, R.Watkins, G.Woodcock, K.Brambley, (reserve, M.Cain).

The girls Netball team (pictured above) won the 'Small Schools Trophy' for gaining the highest points amongst the smaller schools.

Their team was (left to right):- D.Solley, Y.Lunn, K.Webb, W.Shurgold, J.Brambley, E.Young, L.Cain, J.Waring, S.Trim."

(Froyle Newsletter, April 1978)

In June Froyle, as the previous year's winners, played host to the annual Knock-out Competition.

"The Knock-out Competition was held on Treloar's field.... Mr Peters organised the games, Col Willcocks gave a running commentary over the loud speaker system and Revd Daubney presented the prizes. This year Froyle came third, with Bentley winning."

1979 had its share of problems. The weather was very severe at the start of the year and there was also an oil shortage, due to a tanker drivers strike, with teachers wondering how they would get to school without a car - many of them now lived quite a distance from their school. Mrs Woolford resigned from the kitchen at the end of the year and Mrs Trim became school cook in January 1980, with Mrs K.Hart as kitchen helper. Miss Booker left the school at the end of the Summer Term but she was replaced by a newly-trained teacher, Mrs J.Lewis.

Annette Eyre, nee Fry, (1977-1983) remembers this particular school photo.

"I wouldn't smile because my two front teeth were missing!", she said. Obviously the photographer said something amusing to make her feel less self conscious, because Annette, seen here in the second row, far left, of this 1979 group, has one of the prettiest smiles you could hope to see. Like most children who attended Froyle School, she has mainly happy memories, although the outside toilets were certainly not amongst them!

"They were so cold and dark and dingy. We never went into the far one as that was darker than ever."

Annette and her best friend, Natalie Solley, also pictured above, front row, second from right, were absolutely certain that the bell-tower was haunted. "We just knew it was." Annette said with feeling!

Educational changes continued. The Taylor Report, concerning Religious reforms and management, came into being, followed by meetings and discussions.

Mrs Julie Jones with her Infant class of 1979

Mrs Nora Jupe with her Upper Juniors class of 1979

There was more in-service training incorporating the use of the new County R.E. handbooks. Finance became more difficult; schools were given a lower telephone allowance and even school windows were to be cleaned less often!

As a result of the Primary School Report, a National Primary School Survey was inaugurated, with every school in the country sending in details of its aims, objectives, organisation and curriculum; also any future plans for the school. This all took much more of teachers' time, both in and out of school hours. It was intended to give the teachers a clearer idea of where they were going - or hoped to go! For some years, schoolwork had become less formal with topics and projects particularly replacing the 'Three R's'. There were more modern methods of learning tables and spellings, and reading schemes sprang up in large numbers; publishers produced many educational games and kits, and concern began to spread whether educational standards might have fallen? The 'Fourth R', Religious Education, was now of greater importance, but Language, as opposed to just Reading and Writing, was also a priority. Maths reform was yet to come!

At his annual visit this year, the dentist was very concerned with the state of the children's teeth, comparing unfavourably with those of children in neighbouring schools, so it was decided to ban sweets on school premises for the time being. The wisdom of this decision was reinforced when the dentist later reported considerably less treatment required.

School milk and meals had caused problems in 1980. Since the Second War, free milk had been provided to all school children, but at the beginning of the financial restraints was now only available to Infant children. Some schools introduced a private milk scheme so that Junior children could purchase their one third pint each day, and when in April all free milk ended, except for needy children, the Froyle scheme applied to all the children for a while until later they were able to purchase a milk-shake from the school meals service.

Of more concern was the announcement that school meals would rise from 35p to 50p per day. Prices had been gradually rising but this was a sharp increase and meant that parents would have to find 75p extra per week for each of their children, the alternatives being to send the children with sandwiches or take them home at lunchtime.

This was the beginning of the decline of the School Meals Service which must have been a worrying financial burden to the authorities, as only the cost of the actual food had been covered by the children's contributions. Older staff looked back regretfully to the days of 'meat and two veg', followed by tarts or puddings that remained mouth-watering memories, but the days of tablecloths, table service and flowers on the table had gone for ever! The sandwich children were provided with a plate, knife and a glass of water, and were allowed to bring a hot drink, provided it was in a suitable container, in winter. Worse was to follow and when the plate etc. was withdrawn, children were expected to eat their lunches out of sandwich boxes! Although the majority of children opted for sandwiches at first, there was a drift back to the school meals, but now they consisted more and more of 'convenience' foods with reduction of kitchen hours and sometimes staff numbers. There was talk in many counties of privatising the system and many schools went over to buffet or cafeteria service, but Froyle School was lucky to keep its cook, kitchen helper and supervisory assistant until its closure in 1986.

Mrs June Trim worked at Froyle School from 1979 until 1986.

"I started working at Froyle School as kitchen helper in December 1979, then took over as cook-in-charge in 1980, staying with the school until it closed. When I started work we were preparing in excess of 50 meals per day but with dwindling numbers, I was only preparing 22 meals per day when the school closed. We were lucky in that a large percentage of children had school meals with only a few having packed lunch.

For my first term I was preparing and serving full roast dinners and cooked puddings every day, however after the Easter term all meals changed and we were no longer allowed to buy joints of meat or allowed to cook puddings, serving instead pies, fish fingers, chips etc. and for puddings we served yoghurt, ice cream and instant whip.

My day started at 8.30am, when my first job was to light the oven and fill and switch on the steriliser. In the latter years I did not really need to light the oven so early but in the winter, as the kitchen had no heating, other than an electric fire up on the wall, I used the oven to help warm the room. We served lunch at 12.05 after first having to put out and lay the tables. After lunch I did my paper work - I had to do the menu for four weeks at a time. I ordered the provisions for the next weeks meals on a Thursday.

Most schools had deliveries two or three times a week but as ours was only a small school we only had one delivery a week, so I had to make sure that I had not forgotten anything, although the other

Cook, Mrs Trim, taking part in the school's pancake day celebrations in 1984

schools in the district were always willing to help out in the case of an emergency. The work was good, although it could get rather fraught. I have, however, many happy memories of the children and things they said and did.

When I first became cook I had never used instant potato, so I made it up as best I could adding salt and water. I then made duchess potatoes cooking them in the oven, however it turned out that salt had already been added, also I had added too much water so they cooked hard and flat and very salty. As Mrs Jupe had a rule that no one was allowed to leave anything they had put on their plates I went to her and told her that the duchess potatoes were horrible and if the children did not want them could they leave them, however I need not have worried the children loved them and kept coming back for more. Mrs Jupe had to bring in an order stopping children coming up for more than seconds as the lunch sessions were getting longer and longer.

On another occasion I realised that I had not made enough dumplings so quickly made some more, forgetting to add the raising agent. Hoping for the best, I served them and all seemed well until during a lull in conversation a little voice piped up, 'Mrs Trim, your dumplings are like bullets.'

I did have some successes however! On one occasion I had been talking to the secretary about Yorkshire puddings and had jokingly said that my puddings rose so well they reached the roof of the oven. A week or so later I had to call her into the kitchen as the puddings had literally stuck to the roof of the oven and I had to cut them out with a knife!

After work I went into the school and helped the children with cooking art and towards the end of my time at the school I became a special needs assistant helping children with learning difficulties. I had some lovely times working with the children."

Getting down to some serious pancake making in 1984

At the end of one Christmas term June and a group of children had to make a Christmas cake for the school party. "Having made it, the next job was to ice and decorate it. Mrs Jupe had bought some silver balls and came up with an idea whereby each child was given some of the balls and a straw - the idea being to suck up the ball onto the end of the straw and place it on the cake. I will leave you to imagine what else landed on the cake as well as the silver balls, however the cake was duly presented and enjoyed by a large number of people."

1980 was a restricted year for education generally. Financial cuts were biting, staffing ratios had to be cut, the Primary Survey was causing much extra work and worry and enquiries continued about standards and curriculum in schools, both by the government and the public at large. By the Autumn the forecast of school numbers at Froyle was 50 or under, and so the Area Education Officer notified the school in April that one teacher must be redeployed in September. As Mrs Lewis lived in Winchester and wished to work nearer home, it was arranged for her to be redeployed to a Winchester school. Later in the Summer Term however, Mrs Jones accepted her promotional post at Four Marks, the appointment having been 'frozen' for some time, and this meant that the school would lose two teachers but only appoint one in their place, from the redeployed list. This naturally meant that parents were very concerned over their children's future; they held meetings with governors, as managers were now called, and with the A.E.O., but the only concession granted was extra help on one morning each week for children with special needs.

In September the Infant Class was taken by Miss C.Tulk, a redeployed teacher who lived in Winchester and would therefore have a long bus journey to reach school each day. This lasted only one term, as Miss Tulk wished to move back to Winchester, but as there had been a disruption to the Infant Class particularly, from half-term onwards, Mrs C.Taylor returned, to work part time with some of the children until Christmas, and then to take over the Infant Class in January 1981.

The passing of the 1981 Education Act meant the acceleration of curriculum updating during the year, with a special emphasis on Mathematics. Assessment procedures were studied and the new record system installed. Hampshire children aged 7, 11 and 14, now took 'Cognitive Ability Tests' in addition to those they had already used or wished to use; there was now more liaison between Eggars School and with Bentley School.

Much help was now given to the school by parents and friends and this meant that the children were able to work in small groups and very often get individual attention and everyone was very grateful for their kindness.

In the Summer Term of 1981 there was much excitement over the wedding of the Prince of Wales and Lady Diana Spencer in July. In celebration of the event, the children staged a 'Celebration of Weddings' afternoon in school.

A Celebration of Weddings, July 1981
From l to r: Wayne Collingbourne, Adrian Trim, Shaun Binfield, Fiona Elliott,
Helen Burras, Sharon Tilley, Sally Andrews and Nicholas Sinnott

Beginning with descriptions of weddings around the world, the youngsters told their invited 'wedding guests', parents and friends of the school, about Sikh, Buddist, Moslim, Hindu and Jewish wedding ceremonies before showing them a typical Christian wedding with 11 year old Fiona Elliott as the blushing bride and Sean Binficld, also 11, as the groom. The Vicar, Reverend Kenneth Daubney, went through the wedding service with the children, explaining the meaning of each part. At the end of the afternoon the usual presentation to school leavers was made by Lt.Col.Willcocks, chairman of the governors.

1981 closed with 'Bob Cratchitt's Christmas', 'St. George and the Dragon' (mummers play) and a repeat performance of 'Christmas in Mexico' as a tribute to Mr Lark's (right) continuous musical efforts and expertise, which had been appreciated by both staff and children alike. He had retired that year from teaching, after 7 years service as peripatetic teacher at Froyle School. Retirement was not to sever his connection with the school however and he returned on a voluntary basis until it closed.

Mrs Taylor with her Infant class of 1981

Mrs Jupe with her Junior class of 1981

Carols round the piano at Christmas 1981

Prizewinners at the Flower Show in 1982
with Mr Hawkins (left), Mrs J. Bootle-Wilbraham and Mr Hart

1982 saw the school running its own Flower Show in May with the help of Mr Hart and Mr Hawkins and the P.T.A. organising an Auction Sale in the Village Hall. Mrs Pat Morris, a governor, was the auctioneer and the event raised £200 for the school.

'Moving House', a project undertaken in November 1982

During the year there had been a check on the safety of the bell-tower, the redecoration of the school kitchen and the repair of the playing field fence. The Rodent Officer safely eradicated mice from inside the school, and the P.E. shed was fumigated because of rats. The 'powers that be' had begun to realise that delay in work on buildings might prove very costly in the future, and the request for some school interior decoration was not turned down at the end of the year.

School governors played a greater part in school affairs in 1983, apart from regular meetings, they joined headteachers at Eggars for a meeting on the implication of the 1981 Act. They visited the school as individuals but also as a group they were responsible for 'vetting' the school's 'Curriculum Review' before it went to the Area Education Officer.

In May the Vicar, Reverend K. Daubney, had retired from the parish; he was presented with a picture of the Chartres 'Virgin Mary' window from the school at his farewell. The Reverend K.Bachell succeeded as Vicar now of both Holybourne and Froyle and he continued the school visiting.

Mrs Taylor resigned and left the school in 1983 and was replaced by Mrs Rosemary Russell. At Mrs Taylor's farewell, the children performed 'The Evening Star', based on radio broadcasts during the term, Mr Lark helping with the music.

Mrs Russell took up her duties in September 1983, taking on responsibility for computer work. After a talk by Mr Peter Wyles, headteacher of Bentley School, at the P.T.A.'s A.G.M., money was quickly raised in the village for a school computer. A video recorder was given to the school from area funds.

Although at the start of 1984 the school seemed to be flourishing, and about to be redecorated, there were rumours of closure throughout the year. In the second half of the Spring Term however, to everyone's surprise and for the first time in about fifteen years, the school was partly redecorated and this was followed by an offer from the parents to help with more decorating during the Easter holiday, under the guidance of Mr Whittock. The school was now a much more pleasant place to work in. Indeed, the P.T.A. helped the school throughout the year and a '50 Club', with up to 50 members paying £1 a month, was formed with a monthly draw of three prizes. This proved very popular and raised much needed money for the school funds.

1985 was to be the last full calendar year for Froyle School, starting with very snowy weather which disrupted school activities. The County Education Committee decided at their meeting that the school should close in July 1986 and accordingly notices were sent to the school to be prominently displayed for two months, to enable any objections to the scheme to be made. As letters of objection required ten signatures, this restricted objections to governors, staff, the P.T.A. and a few others.

On February 4th a public meeting had been held in the school, with Mr Slade, the Area Education Officer, accompanied by Mr F.Carswell, Senior Primary Advisory Officer, addressing the meeting, which was crowded with governors, staff, parents, villagers and other interested people. During the Spring Term the future of teaching and ancillary staff was discussed but there was great uncertainty for many more months to come. Bentley would become the designated school for ex-Froyle pupils, but the parents could opt for other schools, particularly Holybourne, which was 'Aided' and could take children within a ten mile radius of the school, also traditionally, since its foundation 200 years before, three places were reserved for pupils from Froyle village there.

The final closure proposal was not validated until September when letters, first to the P.T.A. secretary, then to the chairman of governors, were received and a copy of the governors letter was sent to the school. In November the County Education Officer, Mr R.Clark, visited the school, spending the afternoon with children and staff, who were able to discuss their worries with him. Bentley School now made enquiries for the use of the Froyle premises for one year after July 1986, so that proposed alterations and extensions to Bentley School could be made more quickly and safely.

After the final closure notice, parents and teachers were determined to make sure the last two terms of Froyle School were to be happy successful ones. The P.T.A. organised a 'Car-Boot Sale' for funds and at the A.G.M. they organised an illustrated story competition, for both Infants and Juniors. The stories were put on the computer by the children and the printouts mounted with the illustrations, anonymously of course. A bass xylophone was purchased from school funds, after consultation with Bentley School, where Mrs Russell hoped to transfer after July 1986. Mrs Jupe had already decided to retire when the school closed.

As Christmas approached the usual excitement was tinged with sadness. For the last time children were helped to make Christmas cakes, puddings and mincemeat and the school acted a final Nativity tableau on the last day of term. That same evening the staff invited the governors to a Christmas Dinner, in appreciation of their help throughout the year.

1986 was also to be very busy. Plans were made to 'go out with a bang' with many farewell activities before the closure. The curriculum was maintained, also the testing, so that pupils' records could be completed ready for transfer, and final reports could be taken home.

Just as preparations were being made for the main 'Farewell Occasion', the Architects Department of the County finally decided that the bell-tower was unsafe - the staff had worried about this for several years. Scaffolding was erected and the bell-tower removed, the bell and weather vane being rescued for the final exhibition. Luckily the scaffolding was removed just before the 'Farewell Days' but the school looked rather sad without its turret.

"There was a school closure, so that Mr & Mrs Booth, members of staff and the PTA committee, could prepare the school for the 'Farewell Occasion' tomorrow. A photographic exhibition was arranged by Mr & Mrs Booth (below) in the school hall, with appropriate exhibits for each decade of the school's history...."

(Friday, 20th June)

For more than thirteen hours on Saturday 21st June, some six hundred visitors came to take part in a pleasant but sad reunion on a perfect summer's day. Many memories were revived, prompted by the photographic exhibition in the Hall of the school's history in decades, which we had mounted. It had taken several months of collecting and recording the materials and contacting past pupils and that information and those photographs were to form the basis of the book you are now reading. In the Junior Classroom, children's work over the past decade was displayed. Sustained by ploughman's lunches and cups of tea, some visitors stayed all day and enthusiastically joined in the dancing displays in the afternoon. After a tea party for the school children and a disco for the teenagers, the grown-ups enjoyed a barbecue and disco and

May Cooper finds herself on the 1923 Maypole picture

were loathe to go home until just before midnight when a thunderstorm broke - the school really did close with a bang!

On Friday, July 11th, Mrs Jupe's 60th birthday, she wrote in her log book,

"There was a school closure today so that the staff could clear up ready for the Farewell Service and official closure of the school on Monday and they held a farewell lunch in school."

That Farewell service on the following Monday was held in St Mary's Church,

"......the Farewell Service was held in church, when past and present pupils were joined by staff, governors and many parents and friends in a thanksgiving and tribute to over one hundred years of education at Froyle School."

Mrs Dean, a past headteacher and Lt.Col.Willcocks, chairman of the governors, spoke about the school and the children performed their play, 'The Conversion of Saul', as the theme of the service was 'Light'. Froyle School ended as it had begun, with a service in church and tea in the school.

After presentations had been made to Mrs Jupe and the staff, by Mr Roger Haddock, the Assistant Area Education Officer, and autograph albums had been

Mr Roger Haddock, the Assistant Area Education Officer, presents Mrs Jupe with the "Gold Letter", a token of the County's appreciation

presented to the children, containing a copy of their last school photograph, the cake sculpted by Mrs Trim in the shape of the school building was cut and eaten.

After this a photographic record of the 'Farewell Occasion' was presented to Mr & Mrs Booth and the gathering dispersed, Mrs Jupe clutching the giant basket of flowers presented to her. The Reverend P.Welch had previously made Diocesan presentations to all the staff and wished then well.

All that now remained was the final clearing up and preparation of the school for Bentley's use in the Autumn. On Wednesday, July 16th 1986, as the children gathered on the front lawn for the last time, parents joined them for a short meeting where Mrs Jupe, who was retiring that day, supervised the youngsters as they presented their farewell gifts to the staff. Finally, Mrs Jupe thanked everyone for their help and co-operation and expressed the hope that they would all retain happy memories of the school for many years to come. She finally closed the school with the words,

> *"It only remains for me to now say 'goodbye' and 'thank you' as our*
> *Froyle school children leave Froyle School for the last time."*

Those were also the last words written in the log book of Froyle Primary School.

Two 'snaps' from Mrs Jupe's Photo Album

Cycling Proficiency Certificate holders in 1976, with Mrs Bennett and Mrs Pritchard

Enjoying a Residential Visit to Minstead in September 1979

The Class of '86

The very last official school photograph

In the June before Froyle School's official closure Chris Booth took this final group photograph as Mrs Jupe wanted a picture of that 'Class of 86' to give to each of her pupils at the Farewell Service, along with an autograph book.

The Class of '86

Back Row, left to right: Mrs June Trim, Mrs Sylvia Gould, Mrs June Wright, Mrs Sonia Hall, Mrs Rosemary Russell, Mrs Nora Jupe.

Third Row: Mark Sealey, Nicholas Hawkins, Timothy Wood, Paul Jerram, Paula Gould, Michelle Greaves, Kevin Bellis.

Second Row: Lee Smyth, Richard Wells, Victoria Hawkins, Vicky Bellis, Emma Fulleylove, Daniel Wells, Matthew Fulleylove.

Front Row: Lisa Tilley, Elizabeth Clark, Louise Robinson, Melanie Gould, Nichola Gould, Samantha Bulpitt, Richard Peters, Arron Graham.

To be more precise this is one of 36 photographs taken by Chris that day. Mrs Jupe had asked for 30 copies of the photo, so Chris simply took a whole film, while Annette did her best to persuade everyone to sit still and smile for all 36 frames. As a result, each photograph is unique!

And where are they now, that 'Class of '86'? We caught up with five of them and asked them what they were doing now, as well as their memories of Froyle School.

Louise Robinson

My main memories of Froyle school (which aren't very extensive considering my age when it closed) are of when we had snow, and sometimes there would be a big snow drift over the front door, and I could never forget the outside toilets which were always freezing, and the locks used to frequently ice up in very cold weather. The older children always used to tell us that they were haunted! When there was snow we all used to ask to go to the toilet so that we could go outside and have a quick snowball fight, but it didn't take Mrs Russell long to cotton on!

I also remember the big tree trunk that all of the older kids used to be allowed to play on, but whilst I was there I was always too young, and the one time I did manage to sneak on I fell off, made a hole in my new tights and grazed my knee quite badly - it was worth it though! I definitely remember being very upset when we were told that the school was going to close, but I was also quite excited that I would get to go on a minibus to Bentley School, instead of on the child seat on mum's push bike!

After finishing my primary education at Bentley, I went on to Eggars where I got my GCSE's. I then went to Alton College where I left with 3 A Levels in Art, Media Studies and English Literature. I got a place at my first choice of university (the University of Gloucestershire - based in Cheltenham) from where I graduated in November 2002 with a 2:1 in Professional Media with Advertising.

During College and University I have had several part time jobs including painting at Porta Romana in Froyle, lifeguarding at Alton Sports Centre, and waitressing at the races in Cheltenham. I am now living in Putney in London pursuing a career in Interior Design, starting with the complete refurbishment of my flat!

Dan Wells

I can actually remember the day my mum made the phone call for me to start. It was one of my unhappiest memories! As for happy memories, Christmas was always fantastic at Froyle. Being that young it was so exciting. I remember we were allowed to bring toys to school as it approached. And the final school day before Christmas we played games and had a special Christmas dinner. Whilst we all waited anxiously with our Mums and/or Dads in the main hall, we would hear the jingle of reindeer bells. Then the door opened and Father

Christmas appeared. Faces lit up in anticipation to greet the bearer of gifts. I'm sure Mr Lark was always Father Christmas.

I remember one day how Mr Lark, who was also our pianist, saved our bacon! A few of us dared someone to throw a beanbag (the type we always used for sports day) at a picture which stood high above the Junior classroom blackboard. Now this picture was of the Queen, who I think Mrs Jupe respected highly. After realising our mistake AND being caught in the act by Mr Lark, panic set in! But the point was, he casually put the picture back and didn't say a word. I've never forgotten that.

I also remember maypole dancing, when myself, Shane Collingbourne, Andrew Scott and Richard, my brother, would sit on the middle section as we didn't want to dance.

On leaving Froyle Primary School I continued my education at Eggars Secondary School, followed by a year at Guildford College of Technology where I completed a graphic design course. After that a year at Alton College where I retook my GCSE's due to my tomfoolery previously. I then completed a two-year GNVQ Advanced Business studies Diploma.

Whilst I studied at Alton College, I used my summer breaks for two consecutive years to work in a summer camp in the Adirondack Mountains, which is located in New York State, about five hours from Canada. Once camp had finished I used some quality time to explore the east side of the States on both visits to camp. My first experience of full-time work was at Porta Romana (Interior Designers based in Froyle) with my old school friend Lee Robinson. Previous part-time work whilst in education included washing dishes at the Prince of Wales Public House; bar service, and I also worked weekends and holidays at Avenue Nurseries Garden Centre at nearby Lasham where my eldest brother Gareth still works. After Porta Romana I left the nest in search of a job in Brighton living in a student filled house. Brighton is a lovely place but the jobs were scarce and I felt I was in the wrong place. I dashed home to the nest to receive a phone call from a friend I had met in London, who had asked if I fancied a crack at a job up in town. Luck had landed on my doorstep from that destiny-aimed call. I've always been a creative person, so the company I began employment for nearly 6 years ago was exactly the place for me. I never really knew what I wanted to do so this was indeed a godsend.

My company is called Tag Creative and I'm a Scanner Operator and Mac Retoucher. We deal with large advertising agencies throughout the world including Amsterdam, and New York to name a few. Adverts I've worked with include Nike, Siemens, Vodafone, L'OREAL, and I could bore you further, but I fear my life is now up to date.

Lizzie Clark

My parents moved to Lower Froyle a few months before I was born and my first year at school was spent at Froyle, the school's last year. I remember the lovely views over the fields behind the school, sports day in the field over the road, being a mouse in the Taylor of Gloucester and walking home through the "Beeches" on nice days. Mrs. Jupe was the headteacher and Mrs. Russell taught us. The youngest all had "word tins" in which were cards with new words to learn at home. The building was beautiful.

The school stayed open a year after it officially closed to accommodate the Bentley school pupils whilst that school was being extended, then we all moved to Bentley.

Having attended Bentley, Eggars and Alton College I am now in my final year studying Law at Southampton University.

Victoria Hawkins

I do remember being very happy at Froyle School. At the time it was just school and therefore a drag, but in hindsight I had a great time! When I talk to other people about their primary schools, I realise that in many ways we were lucky to go to such a small village school. Some of my stories about school make it sound like a 1950s novel! I do remember Mrs Jupe giving us money to go to shop once and buy ice-lollies for everyone on a particularly hot day, I don't think that would happen in many schools. I think the memories that have really stuck always involve special days like Halloween, Christmas, Sports Day, and of course the maypole dancing. There seemed always to be a lot of dressing up - I particularly remember a play about spring, where I had to dress up as a Roman goddess with a lot of chiffon scarves hanging from me. However, I did seem to leave school without knowing my times tables, but I don't think it's really ever done me any harm!

After completing a degree at York University and then an MA in History of Architecture at the Courtauld Institute in London, I spent some time working in Alton for a language training company, producing English Language Teaching text books and later an on-line English course. I then spent a year travelling in Australia, South-East Asia and India. I've now been living in Oxford for just over a year, working in ELT publishing for Oxford University Press.

Tim Wood

"I would imagine my first day at Froyle Primary School was much like that of many others. I had been excited for weeks, looking forward to making new friends and taking the next big step towards growing up. I remember wearing a new uniform, carrying a green satchel and being strapped into a shiny black pair of school shoes. I say a new uniform; in fact it consisted of a mixture of amended hand-me-downs, including a pair of shorts. Why is it that mums insist on sending their sons to their first day at school in shorts?

The day began with the utmost excitement intermingled with only a little fear. However, once in the car and as the journey slipped by, the excitement subsided and the fear grew, larger and larger, until... aaaahh – utter panic! No, don't want to go anymore – going to cry... A few minutes later, deposited by a stern mother and confronted with the engulfing warmth of my first ever schoolteacher, Mrs Taylor, I found myself plonked amongst a sea of friendly faces, blissfully drawing away at a picture of my house, my garden and my family. This school business wasn't so bad after all...

To be honest, there aren't too many isolated incidents that I remember from my time at Froyle, principally because my career there was so short-lived. Not long after joining, the last remaining twenty or so of us were rounded up and herded in with the mob from Bentley. When that happened, we admittedly remained at Froyle for a while whilst the premises at Bentley were extended to accommodate the extra numbers, but inevitably the real Froyle Primary School as we knew it had disappeared.

Having said that, though, I certainly do remember the looming figure of Mrs Trim, one of the formidable dinner-ladies, bashing out my first ever school dinner: bangers, mash and beans! I also have fond memories of Christmas time. The school was decorated in paper-chains and other decorations that we'd spent hours licking and sticking together. There was also a big red letterbox that we'd all made in an afternoon's frenzy of Blue Peter-style cutting, gluing and painting, and in the run up to Christmas we used it to post our Christmas cards to each other. On the last day of term we sang carols in front of the mums and dads and were given variety boxes of Cadbury's chocolates.

Slightly less fond memories involved the dreaded maypole and Morris dancing practices. Even at that young age, I was fully aware that there was something not quite right about prancing about with ribbons and jingling bells... Perhaps my fondest recollections, however, surround the orange carpet. At the end of the large oblong-shaped classroom with its bare wooden floors and cold metal and plastic tables and chairs, like a warm island, there was an expanse of orange carpet. It was here we would sit and play the recorder or learn new words that we would write out neatly on bits of card and keep in our 'Golden Virginia' smoking tobacco word-tins. Best of all, though, at the end of the day, Mrs Taylor would sit us all down and tell us a story for fifteen minutes. I don't think there was anything more blissful than sitting cross-legged on the orange carpet, with the sun streaming in through the big sash windows and being carried away into the realms of animal kingdoms and make-believe adventures.

Aside from these little remembrances, the only other recollection I have left comes from a kind of blend of impressions and feelings that were accumulated over time by my different senses. It is really the physicality of my time at Froyle that has stayed with me, and interestingly, this is defined by the seasons of the year.

In autumn, I can remember the dewy grass and the low fog hanging just above the football pitch on the rec as we trooped our way along the couple of miles up to school from Lower to Upper Froyle. This took us past Westburn Fields and in to the Beeches, where the golden beech leaves swirled and whooshed around our ankles. Once in the playground, the Yew trees scattered their mushy red berries and the horse chestnut trees not only shed their leaves, but also their spiky green shells which were filled with those treasures that would yield hours of hearty conker duels.

In winter, I can recall the heavy frosts, icicles hanging from the trees and the plumbing in the outside 'bogs' being all frozen up. We all seemed to wear duffel coats with a piece of elastic threaded through from one sleeve to the other and a woolly mitten hanging from each end. The school took on that damp, musty smell and looking out the window, the sky was almost always a swirling metallic grey, punctuated only with the black fingers of the leafless trees in the distance.

Spring brought the steady onslaught of Hampshire's finest green countryside. I can remember going on 'nature trips' during this time, when we would set out to observe the blooming daffodils in March or the drooping bluebells in May, and identify the different types of tree as they exploded with light green shoots and buds. Preparing the bark rubbings and flower pressings we'd taken was the order of the day on our return to the classroom, we then scribbled a few explanatory words below before we hung them up around the class.

Summer was inevitably the most enjoyable time. Everything seemed to speed up as we rushed around the playground playing football and 'it'. The big horse chestnut in the centre of the playground would be laden with lush greenery, the long fields out the back looking towards Yarnhams would be waving with golden wheat and the sky would be a never-ending deep blue. The highlights of the summer term would be the rounders matches and sports day, with the sack race, the egg and spoon race, the sprint and the Mums and Dads races.

Although my memories of Froyle Primary School are brief, I would say that all the same my time there has had a profound effect on the sort of person I am today. Going to school in such a modest and beautiful setting made for a very happy early childhood, which in turn laid the best foundations for later growing up. I believe there aren't very many of these kinds of true village primary schools left in this country now and accordingly, I feel very grateful to have been blessed with such an educational grounding.

I graduated from University College, London, last summer; I managed a 2:1 from a four year course reading Spanish and Portuguese which included a year in South America. Having now decided to follow a career in the law, I am currently in my first year of two at Guildford Law College. After this I have a contract lined up with a law firm in London."

Postscript

Hugh Stanford, of Wellar Eggar, places the 'Sold' notice on Froyle School in 1988

Ａnd so one hundred and eighteen years of education came to an end in the village of Froyle. Well, that's not entirely true, of course, as Bentley School took over and used the building, with the addition of a temporary classroom, for a further year, while its school was enlarged to cope with the influx of Froyle children.

In July 1987 the school was handed back to the Treloar Trust, from whom it had been leased. The Trust considered incorporating it into the rest of the Lord Mayor Treloar College, but after discussion, decided to put it on the market.

One year later, on July 8th 1988, Froyle Village School came under the hammer of Weller Eggar Auctioneer Mr 'Jumbo' Fuller. With planning permission for change to a single dwelling, it was rumoured that the building would reach half a million pounds at auction, but bidding closed at £235,000. The purchasers were local business men Michael O'Leary and Tony Stephensen, who set about turning the old village school into a fine country residence.

A further year passed before "The Old School", Upper Froyle, went on the market, with a price guide of £450,00.

Externally there was little change. Apart from its modern windows the school stands today almost as it must have looked when it opened in November, 1868. It's inside that the transformation has taken place. Gone are the three large stark windows set too high for anyone to look through. In their place are five bedrooms, two of which have en suite facilities, a further bathroom, kitchen, utility room and two reception rooms. The floor has been raised throughout the building by two feet, bringing the large windows down to the level at which the views across the surrounding farmland can be fully enjoyed. The most interesting feature of the house is the main reception room with its gallery (right) and spiral staircase. Throughout the house the false ceiling has been retained, apart from in this room, where the high arched roof trusses have been left exposed. The gallery floor forms the ceiling of the second reception room, making it a good size for a library or studio.

When Tony and Michael bought the property in 1988, 'Jumbo' Fuller told them that they would undoubtedly have plenty of visitors during the conversion. He was certainly right. Tony took so many people round, he lost count. We were certainly amongst those who wanted to see what had become of the old school.

Today it is cherished by it owners, who are in the almost unique position of owning a house whose history has been documented on an almost daily basis from that first day in 1868, when 138 pupils were admitted, to that last day in 1986, when 22 children said goodbye to their school and transferred to nearby Bentley.

As we have seen, one of those pupils was Tim Wood and we make no excuse for repeating his comments about Froyle School, for his words undoubtedly sum up what so many of those ex-pupils feel.

"Although my memories of Froyle Primary School are brief, I would say that all the same my time there has had a profound effect on the sort of person I am today. Going to school in such a modest and beautiful setting made for a very happy early childhood, which in turn laid the best foundations for later growing up. I believe there aren't very many of these kinds of true village primary schools left in this country now and accordingly, I feel very grateful to have been blessed with such an educational grounding."

Froyle School, after conversion, awaits its new owners

Appendix

Working on the B.B.C. Domesday Project in 1985

An Educational Timeline 1868-1986

1869   Endowed Schools Act - encouraging education of girls.

1870   Forster Elementary Education Act - The foundation of our first scheme of national education. Compulsory attendance for children aged 5-12. No religious teaching to be given to any child, if objected to by the parent, in any school assisted by the State. Board schools to be built 'to cover the country with good schools'.

1873   Agricultural Children Act - No child under ten to be employed on the land unless he has attended two hundred and fifty times at a certified school within twelve months. Exam for Labour Certificate for brighter children to leave school early. Register inspection rules tightened.

1876   Elementary Education Act - regulating standards and conditions for leaving school early. No paid child labour under ten years.

1877   First School Attendance Committees formed. Revised Code - school of over 220 pupils needed an adult assistant.

1880   Government education spending reached £2,500,000. Merit Grants encouraged teaching of singing and needlework and imaginative Infant teaching. Compulsory attendance 5-10 and at least part time to 13. Pupil teachers centres increased.

1882   Standard VII introduced. No fees payable from 11 years onwards.

1884   Reform Act - voting rights to most men.

1888   Cross Commission Report - higher standards for pupil teachers and teachers, better attendance recommended, also introduction of domestic science, drawing, woodwork and metalwork.

1890   Revised Code - end of 'Payment by Results'. Drawing compulsory for boys. Physical exercise and games encouraged.

1891   Free Schooling Elementary Education Act. Fees abolished. 10/- grant per child.

1892   Public Libraries Act.

1893   Minimum school leaving age 11 years.

1896   Bryce Report - Central Education Department recommended.

1899   Board of Education established. Minimum leaving age raised to 12.

1902   Balfour Education Act. Local Education Authorities took the place of School Boards and Attendance Committees. Education to be provided through local rates and national taxes.

1905   Prospective teachers were to receive schooling to the age of 16.

1906   Provision of School Meals Act - cheap or free meals to be provided for necessitous children.

1907   School Health Services established.

1908   Childrens Act - posing severe penalties for the neglect or ill-treatment of children. Juvenile Courts established for child-offenders. Free places provided in secondary schools, through scholarship, for a few elementary children.

1913   Board of Education memorandum that girls should take public examinations one year later than boys!

1914	School meals to be available to necessitous children during school holidays if required.
1917	No child labour under 12.
1918	Fisher's Education Act - full time schooling compulsory from 5-14.
1921	Fixed teachers salaries £254-£410. Burnham Committee established.
1922	Government spending on education cut by half.
1924	Cambridge Scheme - primary education to be based on children's interests.
1928	Women gained the right to vote. Experimental television started.
1932	Child Guidance Clinics set up by the Health Service.
1933	Aluminium and early plastic came into use in schools.
1936	Education Act - school leaving age raised to 15. This was not implemented immediately owing to the Second World War.
1937	Health Report revealed one third of the nation's children under-nourished.
1939	War time evacuation of school children to the country.
1940	Evacuation highlighted ill-health of many poor city children.
1941	Provision of school milk and meals becoming universal.
1944	R.A.Butler's Education Act. Fees abolished for secondary schools. Grammar school places as result of 11+ exam. RE made compulsory in curriculum. School leaving age 15, part time day classes until 18. Church schools to be Aided or Controlled. Board of Education became 'Ministry of Education'. Extension of school meals and health services.
1946	Labour government defend the 11+ exam.
1950	School buildings planned more informally.
1957	First Schools TV broadcast.
1959	Crowther Report suggested school leaving age be raised 16.
1960	Teacher training colleges extended to 3 years.
1961	Financial crisis - school building programmes cut. Playgroups and pre-school groups begun.
1964	Schools Council formed. 11+ to be abolished. Corporal punishment queried.
1965	Comprehensive Education now 'official policy'.
1966	Financial crisis - cut backs.
1967	Plowden Report recommended progressive primary methods. Parents recognised as helpful in schools.
1968	Educational spending declared more expensive than defence.
1969	Open University launched. Ideas for new education act asked for by government.
1970	Teacher shortage - 40,000 shortfall. Teachers salaries falling behind those of other professions.
1972	School leaving age of 16 implemented.
1981	Education Act.

Froyle School TImeline 1868-1986

1867   Froyle National Mixed School founded.

1868   Froyle School opens.

1884   New blackboard and easel, handbell, coal scuttle and shovels.

1894   New lights installed. New desks fitted and kindergarten desks supplied.
        Tree lopping and part glass doors fitted to increase light in classrooms.
        School piano provided.

1901   School enlarged - Infant room extended and fitted with new stove and cupboards.
        Playground drainage improved.

1902   School renamed 'Froyle Church of England School.'

1914   Infant room redecorated. Staff room converted into cloakroom.

1923   Maypole presented to school.

1928   Money raised for new school floors.
        New fence between playgrounds and new main school gate.

1932   Supply of water laid on from adjoining schoolhouse.

1948   Large classroom redecorated.

1954   New school cupboard.

1955   'Offices' whitewashed.

1956   Electric lighting installed. Refrigerator for kitchen.

1957   Repairs to roof and windows.   More modern desks.

1958   Complete redecoration of school.

1959   Junior classroom partitioned to provide staff and children's cloakrooms.
        Hand basins and drinking fountains installed.

1960s   Vehicular access provided. Improvements to kitchen.

1964   Flush toilets installed.Ceilings lowered. Solid fuel central heating installed.

1966   Flagstone floors replaced by thermo-plastic tiling.
        Unnecessary chimneys demolished.
        Leaded panes replaced by clear glass. Roof retiled.

1969   School gas meter adapted.

1975   Gas fired central heating fitted.

1977   Holm Oak tree felled.

1982   Safety of school bell-tower questioned.
        Kitchen decorated. Playing field fence repaired.

1984   School partially redecorated. Computer and video recorder acquired.

1986   Temporary classroom erected to cater for Bentley School influx.

The First Attendance Register

Name		Admitted	Age	Residence	Fathers Occupation	Previous Education
Bowers	Harriet	Oct 31	10.7	Yarnham's	Labourer	None
Bowers	James	Oct 31	6.6	Yarnham's	Labourer	None
Bowers	Frederick	Oct 31	4.6	Yarnham's	Labourer	None
Bunce	William	Oct 31	8.0	Lower Froyle	Labourer	None
Bunce	Kate	Oct 31	7.10	Lower Froyle	Labourer	None
Baker	Martha	Oct 31	9.2	Lower Froyle	Labourer	Mrs B School
Beckus	Caroline	Oct 31	8.9	Lower Froyle	Labourer	Mrs B School
Beckus	Daniel	Oct 31	6.0	Lower Froyle	Labourer	Mrs B School
Savage	Eliza	Oct 31	13.0	Lower Froyle	Labourer	Mrs B School
Savage	Ada	Oct 31	6.11	Lower Froyle	Labourer	Mrs B School
Savage	James	Oct 31	4.8	Lower Froyle	Labourer	Mrs B School
Lunn	Frank	Oct 31	9.11	Lower Froyle	Carpenter	Mrs B School
Lunn	Mary Ann	Oct 31	6.6	Lower Froyle	Carpenter	Mrs B School
Lunn	Agnes	Oct 31	5.0	Lower Froyle	Carpenter	Mrs B School
Taylor	John	Oct 31	11.0	Lower Froyle	Labourer	Bentley School
Taylor	William	Oct 31	9.4	Lower Froyle	Labourer	Dame's School
Taylor	Jane	Oct 31	6.2	Lower Froyle	Labourer	Dame's School
Lunn	Kate	Oct 31	12.6	Lower Froyle	Carrier	Dame's School
Smee	Harriet	Oct 31	7.7	Upper Froyle	Labourer	Mrs B School
Adams	Kate	Oct 31	11.2	Upper Froyle	Blacksmith	Mrs B School
Adams	Charlotte	Oct 31	9.3	Upper Froyle	Blacksmith	Mrs B School
Adams	Robert	Oct 31	5.9	Upper Froyle	Blacksmith	Mrs B School
Adams	Frances	Oct 31	4.3	Upper Froyle	Blacksmith	Mrs B School
Adams	Louis	Oct 31	2.7	Upper Froyle	Blacksmith	No means
Jackson	Mary Ann	Oct 31	11.2	Upper Froyle	Gardener	Mrs B School
Jackson	James	Oct 31	7.1	Upper Froyle	Gardener	Mrs B School
Jackson	Alfred	Oct 31	5.4	Upper Froyle	Gardener	Mrs B School
Port	Louisa	Oct 31	8.11	Upper Froyle	Widow	Mrs B School
House	Charles	Oct 31	12.0	Lower Froyle	Blacksmith	Bentley School
Jackson	George	Oct 31	11.0	Upper Froyle	Bricklayer	Bentley School
Port	James	Oct 31	11.0	Upper Froyle	Widow	Dame's School
Lunn	George	Oct 31	8.4	Lower Froyle	Labourer	Mrs B School
Carpenter	Sarah	Oct 31	11.0	Upper Froyle	Gardener	Mrs B School
Carpenter	Letitia	Oct 31	9.5	Upper Froyle	Gardener	Mrs B School
Smith	Alfred	Nov 2	8.0	Lower Froyle	Labourer	Mrs B School
Knight	Elizabeth	Nov 2	10.4	Upper Froyle	Labourer	Mrs B School
Chitty	Minnie	Nov 2	10.2	Upper Froyle	Gardener	Farnham Infant
Knight	Henry	Nov 2	9.2	Upper Froyle	Labourer	Mrs B School
Knight	Emily	Nov 2	6.10	Upper Froyle	Labourer	Mrs B School
Knight	William	Nov 2	4.7	Upper Froyle	Labourer	Mrs B School
Chitty	Ellen	Nov 2	4.11	Upper Froyle	Gardener	No means
Chitty	William	Nov 2	3.6	Upper Froyle	Gardener	No means
Savage	Harriet	Nov 2	8.9	Upper Froyle	Labourer	Mrs B School
Savage	Frank	Nov 2	4.0	Upper Froyle	Labourer	Mrs B School
Hathaway	Agnes	Nov 2	9.1	Upper Froyle	Labourer	Mrs B School
Hathaway	Mary	Nov 2	6.5	Upper Froyle	Labourer	No means
Hathaway	Selina	Nov 2	11.7	Upper Froyle	Labourer	Dame's School
Haddick	Harriet	Nov 2	9.0	Lower Froyle	Labourer	Dame's School
Haddick	Sarah	Nov 2	10.11	Lower Froyle	Labourer	Dame's School
Knight	Annie	Nov 2	8.10	Lower Froyle	Labourer	Mrs B School

Name		Admitted	Age	Residence	Fathers Occupation	Previous Education
Knight	Emily	Nov 2	7.10	Upper Froyle	Labourer	Dame's School
Haddick	James	Nov 2	5.4	Upper Froyle	Labourer	Dame's School
Ellis Long	Thomas	Nov 2	4.4	Upper Froyle	Shopkeeper	No means
Blunden	Martha	Nov 2	11.5	Upper Froyle	Labourer	No means
Blunden	James	Nov 2	9.2	Upper Froyle	Labourer	No means
Blunden	William	Nov 2	7.0	Upper Froyle	Labourer	No means
Blunden	Jane	Nov 2	4.0	Upper Froyle	Labourer	No means
Simpson	Ann	Nov 2	5.1	Upper Froyle	Labourer	No means
Walker	Annie	Nov 2	4.4	Upper Froyle	Labourer	No means
Shirvell	Jane	Nov 2	9.7	Upper Froyle	Labourer	Mrs B School
Shirvell	Louisa L	Nov 2	5.6	Upper Froyle	Labourer	No means
Beckus	Eliza	Nov 2	7.4	Upper Froyle	Labourer	No means
Hebberd	Jane	Nov 2	8.9	Upper Froyle	Labourer	No means
Port	Lydia	Nov 2	9.2	Lower Froyle	Labourer	Mrs B School
Port	Thomas	Nov 2	4.6	Lower Froyle	Labourer	Mrs B School
Gilham	Sarah Jane	Nov 2	8.7	Upper Froyle	Labourer	Mrs B School
Gilham	Noah	Nov 2	6.8	Upper Froyle	Labourer	Mrs B School
Gilham	Martha	Nov 2	4.10	Upper Froyle	Labourer	Mrs B School
Ham	George	Nov 2	7.5	Binsted	Labourer	Mrs B School
Ham	Alfred	Nov 2	6.1	Binsted	Labourer	Mrs B School
Rowell	Georgina	Nov 2	8.4	Lower Froyle	Labourer	Mrs B School
Baker	Annie	Nov 2	7.3	Lower Froyle	Labourer	Mrs B School
Baker	Rosa	Nov 2	4.7	Lower Froyle	Labourer	Mrs B School
Parratt	Mary	Nov 2	11.4	Lower Froyle	Butler	Mrs B School
Goulding	Cicely	Nov 2	9.2	Upper Froyle	Labourer	Mrs B School
Goulding	Thomas	Nov 2	4.2	Upper Froyle	Labourer	Mrs B School
Goulding	Martha	Nov 2	9.8	Upper Froyle	Labourer	Mrs B School
Wingrove	Annie	Nov 2	10.6	Upper Froyle	Gardener	Dame's School
Knight	Charlotte	Nov 2	10.7	Lower Froyle	Labourer	Mrs B School
Knight	Frederick	Nov 2	8.7	Lower Froyle	Labourer	Mrs B School
Knight	Annie	Nov 2	6.7	Lower Froyle	Labourer	Mrs B School
Savage	Annie	Nov 2	5.3	Lower Froyle	Innkeeper	Mrs B School
Mayhew	Ellen	Nov 2	8.2	Lower Froyle	Innkeeper	Mrs B School
Mayhew	James	Nov 2	8.2	Lower Froyle	Innkeeper	Mrs B School
Westbrook	Clara	Nov 2	7.7	Lower Froyle	Farmer	Mrs B School
Westbrook	George	Nov 2	4.0	Lower Froyle	Farmer	No means
Cobb	Sarah	Nov 2	7.5	Upper Froyle	Butler	Mrs B School
Cobb	Annie	Nov 2	4.0	Upper Froyle	Butler	Mrs B School
Baker	Clara	Nov 2	13.6	Lower Froyle	Drayman	Mrs B School
Fullbrook	Robert	Nov 2	9.0	Lower Froyle	Bailiff	Mrs B School
Fullbrook	Esther	Nov 2	7.8	Lower Froyle	Bailiff	Mrs B School
Fullbrook	Lydia	Nov 2	5.9	Lower Froyle	Bailiff	Mrs B School
Baker	Alice	Nov 2	11.6	Lower Froyle	Drayman	Mrs B School
Baker	Charles	Nov 2	9.6	Lower Froyle	Drayman	Mrs B School
Broomfield	Caroline	Nov 2	9.8	Upper Froyle	Innkeeper	No means
Broomfield	Fanny	Nov 2	7.7	Upper Froyle	Innkeeper	No means
Broomfield	Martha	Nov 2	6.0	Upper Froyle	Innkeeper	No means
Clement	Frederick	Nov 2	9.0	Upper Froyle	Coachman	Mrs B School
Stent	Alice	Nov 2	10.0	Millcourt	Keeper	Mrs B School
Stent	Charles	Nov 2	8.0	Millcourt	Keeper	Mrs B School
Stent	Frank	Nov 2	5.0	Millcourt	Keeper	Mrs B School
Savage	Charlotte	Nov 2	5.10	Lower Froyle	Labourer	No means

Name		Admitted	Age	Residence	Fathers Occupation	Previous Education
Kemp	Rosa	Nov 2	8.6	Lower Froyle	Bricklayer	Mrs B School
Hulcoop	Mary Ann	Nov 2	8.9	Lower Froyle	Labourer	Dame's School
Smith	Jane	Nov 2	9.9	Lower Froyle	Widow	Mrs B School
Rampton	James	Nov 2	9.10	Lower Froyle	Labourer	No means
Trimmer	Thomas	Nov 2	6.6	Lower Froyle	Labourer	No means
Trimmer	William	Nov 2	4.0	Lower Froyle	Labourer	No means
Rampton	Jane	Nov 2	10.6	Binsted	Labourer	Dame's School
Rampton	Lydia	Nov 2	8.0	Binsted	Labourer	Dame's School
Rampton	Fanny	Nov 2	6.7	Binsted	Labourer	Dame's School
Wood	Ada	Nov 2	9.10	Lower Froyle	Carpenter	Mrs B School
Kemp	Anne	Nov 2	11.2	Lower Froyle	Bricklayer	Mrs B School
Kemp	Arthur	Nov 2	8.0	Lower Froyle	Bricklayer	Bentley School
Kemp	Ernest	Nov 2	4.6	Lower Froyle	Bricklayer	Bentley School
Stent	Eliza Jane	Nov 2	13.3	Lower Froyle	Labourer	Mrs B School
North	Mary Ann	Nov 2	4.1	Lower Froyle	Labourer	No means
Scrivener	Emily	Nov 2	14.0	Upper Froyle	Woodman	Dame's School
Chappell	Annie	Nov 2	11.0	Upper Froyle	Coachman	Chillam School
Chappell	Mary	Nov 2	12.10	Upper Froyle	Coachman	Chillam School
Chappell	Ada	Nov 2	9.2	Upper Froyle	Coachman	Chillam School
Hamm	Martha A	Nov 2	6.4	Upper Froyle	Gardener	
Neale	Harriet	Nov 2	8.6	Lower Froyle	Labourer	No means. Unable to write
Lakey	William	Nov 2	10.0	Lower Froyle	Labourer	No means. Unable to write
Lakey	Daniel	Nov 2	4.6	Lower Froyle	Labourer	No means. Unable to write
Baker	Bridget	Nov 2	12.11	Lower Froyle	Labourer	Dame's School
Rowell	Jane	Nov 2	4.5	Lower Froyle	Labourer	No means
Taylor	James	Nov 2	6.9	Lower Froyle	Labourer	Dame's School
Taylor	William	Nov 2	4.3	Lower Froyle	Labourer	No means
Parrat	George	Nov 2	11.0	Lower Froyle	Gardener	Mrs B School
Parrat	John	Nov 2	5.9	Lower Froyle	Gardener	Mrs B School
Neale	Frederick	Nov 2	7.8	Lower Froyle	Labourer	Dame's School
Trimmer	Emma	Nov 2	12.0	Upper Froyle	Labourer	Dame's School. Unable to write
Trimmer	Frank	Nov 2	9.0	Upper Froyle	Labourer	Dame's School. Unable to write
Feltham	Alfred	Nov 2	4.8	Lower Froyle	Labourer	Dame's School. Unable to write
Stevens	Frank	Nov 2	7.4	Lower Froyle	Labourer	Dame's School. Unable to write
Baker	Aaron	Nov 2	8.4	Upper Froyle	Labourer	No means
Baker	Mary Ann	Nov 2	7.2	Upper Froyle	Labourer	No means

NOTES

Age: This is given in Years and Months - 7.2 is 7 years and 2 months
Previous Education:
Mrs B School - Mrs Burningham's School at Froyle Cottage, Upper Froyle
Dame's School - various Dame's Schools in the village
Bentley School - adjacent village school
Binsted School - adjacent village school

Index of Names

This index only contains names referred to in the text and may not include
absolutely every occurrence. It is intended as a guide only.
Schoolgirls are indexed under their maiden names